Newsletter Success Secrets

Ian Howlett

Newsletter Expert

Boost your sales, retention, and referrals

www.NewsletterExpert.com

ISBN Paperback: 978-1-9160568-0-0

Revision 58.

Download your FREE quick-start video and time-saving tools

Quick-start video
A summary of this entire book in under 30 minutes.

"The Perfect Newsletter" Checklist
Tick these boxes to make sure your newsletter gets you more sales, retention, and referrals.

"Article Idea Finder" Cheat Sheet
How to get your first 10 article ideas in 10 minutes.

Pre-Flight "Fingers-Crossed" Checklist
The essential final review before sending your newsletter to avoid embarrassing mistakes.

Your questions answered—20 page bonus chapter
FAQ information that changes regularly, included as a free download so it's always up to date. Includes:

- How often should I send my newsletter?
- How can I sell directly from my newsletter?
- Which email software should I use?
- What's a good open rate for an email newsletter?
- How do I keep my newsletter out of the spam folder and the Gmail promotions tab?

Get your FREE video and bonuses now, at
www.NewsletterExpert.com/bonus

············

About the author

Ian Howlett has been producing newsletters since 2011 and has sent literally millions of newsletters on behalf of clients. His newsletters are read by thousands of readers each month, have generated thousands of clicks to sales websites, and bring a measurable, positive return on investment every time they are sent.

He has an MBA with Distinction from the University of Oxford, where he specialised in marketing.

Ian's writing has appeared in major UK magazines including *Autosport* (for motor racing fans), *Pilot* (for private pilots), and *Writing Magazine* (for successful authors and editors).

He has a Private Pilot's Licence and enjoys playing the piano. He lives near Cambridge, England, with Victoria and two huge furry cats called Tom and Jerry.

Want me to help you with your newsletter?

I work with a number of clients to write and distribute their monthly newsletter, in email or in print. To apply for a Strategy Session to see if we could work together, visit:

www.NewsletterExpert.com/call

TABLE OF CONTENTS

....

Introduction

Let me ask you a question: if you could get your customers to spend more, keep your customers for longer, and increase the lifetime value of every customer, what would that do to your profits? And if you could increase your profits, how would that change your business? How would it change your life?

Would you like your customers to keep you and your company top-of-mind when they are finally ready to do business with a company like yours? There is great power in making sure the customer never forgets about you, and knows all the ways in which you can help them.

The three core benefits of a newsletter are sales, retention, and referrals. You can make more sales almost immediately, improve your customer retention to keep customers spending for longer, and increase your referrals to get new customers without spending money on advertising.

A newsletter can help you with all this, and much more besides. The nice thing about a newsletter is that it can be a very self-contained piece of marketing. It doesn't need you to change your world view, or to rethink your whole outlook on life or business. It doesn't need you to scrap your existing marketing. It doesn't need you to make changes to anything else you already do, or change the ways you work. It can be a nice, simple extra thing you can bolt onto what you're already doing.

So if you feel overwhelmed by all the things you feel you "should" be doing, and how they might all fit together, a newsletter is a great place to start.

However, it's not enough just to crank out the first things that come into your head every month.

You need to carefully craft your newsletter as **infotainment**: informative and entertaining in just the right blend. You can think of it as providing intelligent entertainment: serving your own interests by better serving the interests of your customers.

I've meticulously prepared this book to concentrate on discussing the vital principles that nobody else will tell you: these are the things that will lift you head and shoulders above lesser marketers.

You're marketing to your BEST customers

If you're like me, you probably don't read every single newsletter you get. But which newsletters *do* you choose to read? The ones that come from the companies where you're a passionate (or at least interested) customer. These are the companies from whom you're likely to make a purchase, or where you have an ongoing relationship.

In other words: **it's your best customers that read your newsletter**.

For most companies, the classic 80/20 rule applies: roughly 80% of their sales come from the most engaged 20% of their customers. These are the people you're reaching with a newsletter. So don't worry when not every single person on your list reads your newsletter: the people who *will* read it are the people who matter to you most.

What's in this book

I'm going to teach you my proven philosophy of using what I've called a Benefit-Based Newsletter™. Although I include lots of practical nuts-and-bolts advice, this is primarily a book about strategy. I need you to see the big picture, because **the right strategy is what will make the difference between success and failure**.

In part one of this book, I'll show you all the benefits of a newsletter so that you can determine which ones best suit you.

In part two, now you've decided a newsletter is what you need, we look in depth at the 32 major strategic objectives that a newsletter can accomplish, and determine which are the most appropriate for *you*. After all, if you don't know what you're trying to do, how can you do it? We'll cover strategy, and then take a look at the process you can follow to get your newsletter written and sent to your customers.

In part three, we tackle the one big thing that a lot of people worry about, that you absolutely do *not* need to worry about: "But my business is so boring, I don't have anything to say!"

I can guarantee that you have *plenty* to say—certainly more than enough for a monthly newsletter—and I'll tell you exactly what to say in part three of this book. We'll look at the Captivating Categories of Content™ that you need to include, consider headlines and articles in more depth, and look at some ways to hold your reader's attention.

Let's look into the future together for a moment. Imagine what it would be like to be seen as a respected authority in your field: as an expert, not as a salesperson. Think what it would be like to have a platform to regularly demonstrate your knowledge, your credibility, and the results that your products and services can achieve.

Let's get started!

PART 1

THE BENEFITS

CHAPTER 1

The biggest lesson
I ever learned

Let me tell you how a newsletter transformed my life. This is a tale of business mistakes—which I can help you to avoid—and also business successes. There's a big lesson here, as you'll see as you read on.

My name is Ian Howlett. I'm originally from Derbyshire and now I live near Cambridge in rural England. I'm in my forties (crikey!), I love chocolate, and I've had a slightly unusual career.

When I was at school I wanted to be a journalist, so I did my work experience at the local newspaper (yes, we still had them back then). In my teens, I won a national writing competition run by the BBC, and got some of my writing published in an anthology by HarperCollins.

Along with writing, one of my other great interests at the time was computing. I wrote my first computer program at the age of five. That's probably quite old by today's standards, but back in the mid 1980s it was blazing a trail. I made my first online sale in 1995 (of a software library I'd written for a programming language called Visual Basic), which probably makes me an internet pioneer of a very modest sort.

I started using the internet in 1992 (back in the days when it was cool because nobody else knew what it was), and it was starting to become clear from the information that was appearing for free, online, that journalism was going to take a turn for the worse. I didn't want to fall victim to the unstoppable tide of technology that was starting to turn the world of media on its head.

Spotting an opportunity

Fortunately, as you will see later, the perilous and often awful state of today's journalism is actually a great opportunity for business owners like us, because we can fill the gap of providing excellent information that the mainstream media is no longer providing.

However, convinced of the opportunities that computing could offer, and having always enjoyed computer programming, I left the world of writing behind for a while and did a degree in Computer Science.

First lesson: you've got to keep new customers coming in like clockwork

I started my first full-time IT consulting business at the age of 22, with a friend from university. We started off strongly, doing some work on what I believe was the first ever UK newspaper paywall, FT.com (the Financial Times).

We also wrote a travel insurance sales system for an entrepreneur who was leaving a big insurance firm and striking out on his own. Eighteen years later, he is still a client of mine, and that will soon become important in my story here.

Although our projects were successful in this first business, at the time we were better at software development than we were at marketing. We just did a few random acts of marketing, which were sporadic and unreliable. We weren't *consistently* bringing in new potential customers and warming them up, over time, ready for a sale. We just didn't have a methodical and systematic way to do it. We eventually closed down the business (still at a reasonable profit) and went our separate ways.

What they teach you at Oxford Business School

One of the big things in my life was that I always wanted to go to university at either Oxford or Cambridge. Nobody in my family had ever been to university before, but it always struck me as a worthwhile goal to aim for. The idea of being around the sharpest and best minds in the world excited me.

I applied to the University of Oxford to do an MBA, which is a postgraduate business degree. This would let me fulfil a lifetime's ambition, and also hopefully learn how to fix what had gone wrong in my first business. I didn't expect to get in, with something like nine applicants per place, but with a bit of luck and a great big sackful of cash (begged and borrowed from the bank), I was in!

A year of intense work followed: 14 hours a day, seven days a week (sounds like running a business, eh?). I specialised in marketing and consulting and learned from genuine leading practitioners in the field, from companies such as McKinsey and Procter & Gamble (P&G), as well as investment bankers, hedge fund owners, and various entrepreneurs.

Really, what you learn from such an intense experience is the power that comes from a regular, consistent, methodical approach to tackling your work, the mindset shift that comes from being fully-focused and 100% committed, and getting small wins as you chip away at your big goal, day after day.

As an aside, after the MBA I was employed by Oxford University for a while, working on quantum computers.

I worked with Professor Andrew Briggs, a very highly regarded physicist who also happened to be a private pilot who owned a share in a small private plane. We had to give a presentation in Bratislava, so one morning we took off from Oxford at about 6 a.m. and flew all the way across Europe together, then a few days later we flew back over the Alps—incredible! He let me take the controls for a while and I loved it.

Ten years later, in 2017, I became a qualified PPL (Private Pilot Licence holder) myself and I now fly Cessna 172 aircraft based at Cambridge Airport.

Second lesson: you can use regular communication to build a community of loyal customers

About ten years ago, I started a publishing technology company with a couple of other people. We entered it into Seedcamp, a competition run by major venture capital firms, where around 1,000 companies compete each year and around 15 are chosen as winners and receive some investment. We got through the heats and, after a week of schmoozing, we were picked to go on the winners' tour: a three-week visit to some of the biggest internet companies in America, visiting Google, Facebook, LinkedIn, Twitter, Etsy, AOL, Hubspot, and Apple, among others. And yes, I did see Mark Zuckerberg in the flesh!

Our customers were authors and publishers, so naturally we got mentioned in *The Guardian* newspaper, and we built a service that users loved. Once a user joined us, they rarely quit. I was managing the community and I got to know the customers, what they liked, and what they wanted. I learned how to communicate effectively with them.

The magic formula I discovered, that's applicable to newsletters and applicable to *you* in your business, is this: **Communication builds Community**. That's really what you're building with a newsletter: a community of dedicated customers who feel like they're part of something bigger than just being cannon fodder for having "special offers" blasted down their throats.

As shareholders in that company, we differed on how we wanted to take the business forward, so eventually we decided to close it down. We got well over a hundred emails from users who were very sad to see us go. I was overwhelmed by it, to be honest. I still have a collage featuring the images and themes of our company that was handcrafted by one of our customers and sent to us across the Atlantic from America to London, and it hangs in my office to this day.

How many sad emails would *you* expect to receive if you closed down your business? Would *your* customers create a piece of artwork and send it thousands of miles to reach you? (Food for thought—if not, we need to work on that.)

It proved to me that you *can* use consistent and regular communication, that shows you are a company of real human beings in tune with your customer's hopes and aspirations, to build something that has genuine meaning in people's lives.

Here's what's significant: deeper meaning is becoming much more important these days, as people turn away from raw consumerism and look to companies that they can connect with on a more emotional level.

The larger point, and slightly controversial: to some extent and with some people, consumerism and brands have replaced or come alongside religion as an environment where those people will look for, and find, spiritual meaning and significance.

So by using great communication, we were able to build something of significance in our customers' lives, and promote regular, repeat, loyal custom.

My first newsletter got great results

Remember the travel insurance company I mentioned earlier, that I first dealt with many years ago? I'd kept them as a small client, on the side, through all these years. In late 2011, I started writing an email newsletter for them. I'd been doing lots of writing for my previous business, so it seemed like a natural sideline to start.

Sending tens of thousands of emails a month, I experimented with designs, layouts, subject lines, and different types of articles, and with different offers to bring in customers. I soon found a sweet spot, and was able to bring in at least a 5x return on investment (ROI) on each newsletter, even in the slow months (travel insurance is seasonal, like many businesses). That's measuring the return by looking at the actual profit, not the revenue generated (in other words, it includes the cost of goods sold).

And that was just the sales that we could directly track and tie back to the newsletter. Even with the power of online measurement, there are lots of sales that you can't directly track, such as people typing your web address straight into their browser, or phoning you up to place an order.

A 5x return on investment every month

The economics are different for every business, and I could never promise that kind of return to just anyone. Obviously I'm being conservative when I'm giving you these numbers. But I was amazed that with my client's email list, our knowledge of his customers (his readers), a skill for writing articles that readers enjoyed, and an established business with just a small handful of products, we could consistently and repeatedly pull in that sort of money, month after month after month.

This client's newsletter contains many of the features I'll tell you about in this book, and over the years it has brought him many of the benefits that I'll mention in the upcoming chapters.

Over the best part of a decade, the emails I have personally prepared for this client have been sent millions of times. The open rates are way above the industry average, and very few people have ever marked the email as spam. It has proven to be a wonderful and *reliable* marketing investment for him, churning out cash month after month.

How can we get, and keep, customers for life?

If I look back at my whole career, I have now worked with this travel insurance client continually for eighteen years. I have another small business client I have worked with for ten years. I have kept a FTSE 100 client for seven years, when the industry average is around one year at best. In the industries I am in, that's a rare achievement.

For the last couple of years, I have been reflecting intensely on this. How have I managed to keep clients far longer than most people can?

A set of questions has repeatedly gone through my mind:

- How can we get, and keep, customers for life?
- How can we massively increase their customer lifetime value, so a customer is worth at least 10 times more to us than they otherwise would be?
- How can we continually and profitably sell our products and services to them, and have them eagerly coming back for more?

There are many answers to these questions. However, there is one answer that achieves all these aims, and it is absolutely fundamental: **you MUST have a newsletter**.

That's why I have chosen to grow the newsletter side of my business, producing and sending high-quality, fully-customised, profit-generating monthly email and printed newsletters on behalf of my clients.

The big lesson: you've got to have a system

Once you're sure that your company has got a business model that's fundamentally sound, the big lesson is: **you've got to have a reliable and *consistent* system for your marketing**.

That's it. It took me about 20 years of painful experience to learn *and prove* that!

More precisely: **you've got to have a systematic, consistent, trusted, tried-and-tested, repeatable, reliable, never-fails way to perform the following critical tasks:**

- **Leads**: Bring in new potential customers.
- **Warm-up**: Get potential customers familiar with you; get them prepared and ready to buy.
- **Conversion**: Turn these leads into paying customers at the point they're going to buy.
- **Sales**: Keep customers spending money again and again.
- **Retention**: Do everything you can to hang on to the customer by building a lasting relationship with them, based on an emotional connection that would be painful for them to break.

There is one marketing tool that can achieve all of these goals: a newsletter.

CHAPTER 2

The benefits of a great newsletter

We'll quickly cover the basics here. A newsletter is usually a short collection of articles, usually sent once or twice per month, and clearly marked in its title as being a newsletter.

Newsletters can take two main forms: email newsletters or printed newsletters.

An email newsletter is typically sent to all of your customers or potential customers who have opted in and chosen to receive the newsletter.

A printed newsletter is typically A4 size (or US letter size). Any fewer than four pages and it doesn't really feel like a proper publication. Much more than 12 pages and your newsletter starts to become a magazine!

In this book, I will only be talking about newsletters that are sent free of charge to the reader.

So why exactly is a newsletter such a good investment for your business?

A newsletter makes sales NOW!

Although we don't use high-pressure or hard-sell tactics in a newsletter, we can still sell in a soft way—mentioning products, giving a special offer or discount, stimulating impulse purchases, and simply being around when people need us—these all lead to making more sales. Very often, you can *immediately* break even on the sales from the newsletter on the same day that readers receive it. Then the remaining benefits are all free!

A newsletter stimulates referrals by being passed around

In the UK, *Private Eye* magazine claims to its advertisers that it sells 231,073 copies yet has 680,000 readers. Around three times as many readers as there are copies sold! How is that possible? Well, those total readership figures can only be an estimate, but it starts with the magazine coming into a household, and maybe two or three people read it.

The same can happen with your newsletter, spreading your message from existing customers to new prospects who could become customers. It's a type of referral, like word of mouth recommendations.

When someone passes on your newsletter to a friend, it's an implicit recommendation of you, which immediately gains you some trust—after all, who would pass on something from someone they didn't know, didn't like, or didn't trust?

The chances are that your customer will know other people broadly like them, so if the customer is a good fit for your business, their friends are likely to be a good fit for you too.

A newsletter converts prospects into customers by making a first sale

Now that we understand how a prospect might see your newsletter, by having it passed to them by a customer, what happens next? A newsletter can help a prospect who hasn't yet bought from you to get the same feelings of knowing, liking, and trusting you that an existing customer has.

We deliberately engineer these positive feelings when we write the newsletter, and it sets the stage for an easier time selling to new prospects.

The newsletter makes a series of offers to the reader—your prospective customer—and showcases everything you provide. It can often push a prospect into becoming a customer, by making the first sale. Further sales can then flow from this initial response.

A newsletter dramatically cuts your customer acquisition costs

You've seen that a newsletter can get passed along to someone who isn't yet your customer but might well be a good fit to become your customer. That didn't cost you anything. Or they might pick up your newsletter in your place of business. Again, the cost is negligible.

This leads to dramatically lower customer acquisition costs than you could otherwise get.

A newsletter shows the customer everything you have to offer

One of the reasons customers don't buy more from you is that they don't actually know about everything that you offer. A newsletter lets you build awareness and enthusiasm for *all* your offerings.

A newsletter increases customer lifetime value by building relationships

If we can stay in touch with customers then we can keep reminding them that we exist, and keep showing them our new products and services. By building a strong relationship over time, customers can come to feel that they know you, and will come to trust you. This makes them more likely to buy from you and less likely to go to competitors.

A newsletter keeps the customer interested in your category or industry

An important point, often missed, is that we can also keep readers interested in our *category* of product or service. For example, if I ran a fountain pen shop, I wouldn't just mention the pens that I stock myself, I'd be sure to keep you interested in fountain pens *in general*, and everything that goes with them, such as how they're used and things you can do with them. If a customer loses interest in the category, they will lose interest in *you*.

A newsletter keeps you top-of-mind for your customer or prospect

If a customer doesn't hear from you for a while, or doesn't hear about you, they are likely to forget about you! They most likely won't remember who you are, what you do, and what makes you special.

The longer you go without contacting a customer—every month you miss—that customer is getting less and less valuable to you. After 6-12 months, the customer may as well be a stranger to you, as if you'd never done business.

A newsletter lets you hammer home your USP

Your company has things that make you stand out from the crowd, that make you unique. This is your unique selling proposition (USP). Does your customer or prospect know *why* you are unique, and *why* they should do business with *you* rather than any of your competitors?

A newsletter gives you a chance to repeatedly make it clear why *you* are the best choice for them, and why they shouldn't go anywhere else. Month after month, you can reinforce this information.

A newsletter makes sure you're there when the customer is ready to buy

Not all customers or prospects are ready to buy immediately. In fact, most aren't. A newsletter can help keep in regular contact, nurturing the customer or prospect, and repeatedly following up on your behalf without coming across as pushy.

With a newsletter, when the customer is finally ready to make a purchase, you'll be there. Even more importantly, the newsletter has already warmed up the customer and primed them as to why you're the best choice for them, and it's more likely to be you that they will buy from.

A newsletter can have a long shelf life and gets saved for later

I've got printed newsletters from many years ago, which I've kept because they had a good article, or in case they become relevant later. Whenever I come across them, I'm reminded of the company that sent them to me, even if the newsletter was sent almost a decade earlier. If a customer sees something interesting in your newsletter that piques their curiosity, they're likely to save it for later.

Even email newsletters can hang around. I often see my clients making sales from an email newsletter that was sent at least a month earlier. You might think that emails just get immediately deleted, or pushed down the inbox out of sight, but real-world experience shows that this isn't always the case.

A newsletter builds the crucial "know, like, and trust" relationship

As a business owner, you'll have noticed that it's usually easier to sell to an existing customer than it is to sell to a completely new prospect. Why is that? It's because unless things have gone wrong, the existing customer already (to some degree) knows you, likes you, and trusts you. A newsletter can help to further build and strengthen the "know, like, and trust" relationship.

A newsletter sets you up as a credible authority, an expert, and a celebrity

The public perception is that those of us who publish— authors—are experts in our topic. That's the cultural assumption that's ingrained in us.

Here's the thing: your newsletter isn't seen as marketing, it's seen as publishing.

If you have been publishing for a while, and someone has repeatedly seen your name and face in a publication, you become both an expert and a minor celebrity to them, even if it's on a subconscious level. They automatically respect you, and are less resistant to your ideas, methods, and solutions. They are more likely to accept your recommendations as they would accept a prescription from a doctor.

People want to do business with an expert, not with a salesperson. A newsletter gives you that expert positioning.

A newsletter builds your brand without you paying for it

Big brands pay many millions of pounds, every year, to build and maintain their brand image by plastering their logo in as many places as they can.

As small business owners, we can't afford to build a brand that way: we'd go bust before we were anywhere even close to brand recognition with a mass general audience. But we *can* build a brand in the minds of a *targeted* list of customers and prospects by using a newsletter. Consistent, reliable, dependable delivery every month, with your name, logo, colours, and identity, carrying your messages to your intended audience.

You are building recognition and familiarity without spending money specifically just to do that.

A newsletter gives an easy way to show social proof that you can get results

Social proof is just a fancy way of saying that people place value in what they see other people doing. For example, if a restaurant is very popular, most people will assume that it must be good. Star ratings on Amazon are another example of social proof.

By featuring your customers and their testimonials and case studies in your newsletter, you can show your readers that your products and services are widely used, get results, and that you have many happy customers.

Often, people like to do what other people are doing, and buy what other people are buying. They perceive safety in numbers.

A newsletter gives you a proven, successful marketing campaign that rolls out every month like clockwork

A newsletter means you don't have to scratch your head dreaming up ideas for entirely new campaigns every month.

You know that you're going to be covering certain topics in certain ways, and that your audience is ready and waiting to see what you've got to say this month.

In this way, a newsletter takes a lot of the hassle and hard work out of consistent follow-up.

The more times you reach the same person, the more likely you'll catch them when they're ready to buy.

A newsletter keeps people interested in you during slow months of a seasonal or cyclical business

Most businesses have some kind of seasonal or cyclical aspect to them. More books are sold in the run-up to Christmas than are sold at other times of the year. More people go on holiday during the summer than they do in the winter. So you need a way to keep people interested in who you are and what you do—and *remember* who you are and what you do—when it's that time of year when they're probably not going to buy for a while.

By remaining in front of people during these slow times of the year, you'll pick up some sales right away, but you'll keep people warmed up ready for the main buying times of the year.

A newsletter builds value in your business if you're trying to sell or exit

One of the main reasons a company gets acquired, and a main reason the founder is able to sell and cash out, is that the acquiring company is really buying the customer list. They're buying easy and quick access to a known group of good customers.

They're really paying you for the fact that you have gone out and rounded up a high-quality set of customers that are likely to stick around for the long term and be loyal. Your newsletter is key to making that happen.

If your lifetime customer value is high, and your customers stay with you for a long time, it makes your business very valuable to the right acquirer. A newsletter can help you achieve these goals.

Summary: The benefits of a great newsletter

1. Makes sales NOW!
2. Stimulates referrals by being passed around.
3. Converts prospects into customers by making a first sale.
4. Dramatically cuts customer acquisition costs.
5. Shows the customer everything you offer.
6. Increases customer lifetime value by building relationships.
7. Keeps the customer interested in your category or industry.
8. Keeps you top-of-mind.
9. Lets you hammer home your USP.
10. Makes sure you're there when the customer is ready to buy.
11. Has a long shelf life and gets saved for later.
12. Builds crucial "know, like, trust" relationships.
13. Sets you up as a credible authority, an expert, and a celebrity.
14. Builds your brand without you paying for it.
15. Shows social proof that you can get results.
16. Gives you a proven, successful marketing campaign that rolls out every month like clockwork.
17. Keeps people interested in you during slow months of a seasonal or cyclical business.
18. Builds value in your business if you're trying to sell or exit.

CHAPTER 3

Reasons to have an email newsletter

The first question in your mind is probably, "Should I have a printed newsletter or an email newsletter?" Well, my answer would be: do both!

Different people like to read in different ways. Some people prefer email. Some people prefer print (it's not just as simple as old fogeys like print!). Some people have a visual impairment that forces the choice upon them.

If you use both email and print, as a one-two punch, you'll have a higher chance of reaching the right person at the right time.

If you're on a tight budget, email is the cheaper way to go. But you'd be leaving a lot of opportunities on the table.

In this chapter and the next chapter, we'll take a closer look at the pros and cons of email and print for sending newsletters.

You can reach almost everybody with email

You've got an email address, right? So has pretty much everyone else! Compared to any other medium, online or offline, there are very few people you can't reach these days with email. Certainly, there are far more people using email than there are using social media.

Better yet, most people are actually checking their email too. They might ignore their social media accounts for a while, or scroll past lots of old posts if they've not logged into their Facebook or Twitter account for a few days, but most people will check *all* of their emails.

Email is proven to be effective

Marketing superstar Dave Dee sniffed out the following facts about email:

- There are over 6.32 billion email accounts. This figure is predicted to reach 7.71 billion by 2021 which is an increase of almost 22% — Radicati Group (2017).
- 72% of consumers say that email is their favoured conduit of communication with companies they do business with. 61% say they like to receive promotional emails weekly and 28% want them even more frequently — MarketingSherpa.
- 66% of consumers have made a purchase online as a direct result of an email marketing message — Direct Marketing Association.

Email is cheap

Although you have to pay an Email Service Provider (ESP) company such as MailChimp, Aweber, or Infusionsoft to send out your email newsletters, you usually don't have to pay for each email you send.

That's no excuse to be sloppy—although a lot of people are— but it does mean that you can keep a close control on costs, and the costs are relatively low.

Email addresses are easier to collect than postal addresses

It takes a long time to fill in a postal address form, compared to just giving an email address. Although postcode lookups online make this easier, it still feels like a bigger commitment, especially for a prospect who isn't yet a customer. By contrast, you can offer something digital online, such as a PDF or access to a video or webinar, in exchange for an email address.

It's therefore likely that for many businesses, they can build an email list more quickly than a postal address list, and have more people on it.

Email is easy to track

With any of the main email providers, once you've sent your newsletter you can start to see some very useful figures:

- **Open rate**: How many people opened your newsletter, and who exactly were they?
- **Clicks**: How many people clicked a link in your newsletter, and who were they?
- **Interests**: Which links did they click on (so we can track their interests and see what's popular)?
- **Sales**: Who actually bought something? And what did they buy?
- **Revenue**: How much revenue did those sales bring in?

Based on this, we can calculate our return on investment (ROI), and prove to ourselves that our newsletter is worthwhile.

The open rate figures you'll get from email software will under-report the true numbers, because email reading software (like Gmail or Hotmail) doesn't always register that the reader opened the email. However, links that the reader clicked can be accurately tracked, and so can sales figures generated from people who directly clicked those links.

It starts to get a little tricky when a customer sees your email then goes directly to your website, without clicking a link in your email, because you don't know that it's your email that bought them to your site. So most of the time, your email newsletters are actually performing a little better than the figures would have you believe.

We can also track some less happy figures:

- **Bounces**: Whose email address is no longer working?
- **Lost interest**: Who hasn't opened your emails for a while?
- **Abuse**: Who reported you for being a spammer? (You always get the odd one or two, but if it's clear to people why they are on your list then you won't get many spam complaints.)

An email newsletter lets you track your best customers and prospects, to focus your marketing on them

Using a decent Email Service Provider, you can see *exactly* which people have been opening your email newsletters, and which people haven't. Those readers who reliably open every newsletter you send, on the day that you send it, are your hottest customers who are most likely to buy again, or they are your hottest prospects who are likely to buy for the first time.

Once you've figured out who's most likely to buy, you can focus more marketing on them. You could send them some written information in the post, give them a call, or follow up with a sequence of more specific emails (providing you have previously got their permission, of course).

An email newsletter lets you see exactly which products or services a particular person is interested in

If the reader clicks on a specific link in your email newsletter, this gives you even more information. Again, decent email software will let you tag a customer to show exactly which links this reader clicked. You can then see which of your products or services are most interesting to that particular person.

This will let you build more focused marketing campaigns for that customer for those particular items.

An email newsletter reaches people your other marketing emails don't reach

A newsletter doesn't have to be the only email you send to your customers and prospects. It will happily sit alongside other marketing emails you want to send, announcing special offers and other promotions.

People mentally put a newsletter into a different category to other emails, so if you're sending a newsletter along with other emails too, you've effectively got two different types of email trying to reach the target.

A great newsletter is deliberately less salesy than other emails, and will get opened by some people who don't open your other emails.

Email newsletters can still make sales weeks or even months after they are sent

I often see that when I send an email newsletter for one of my clients, we get a rapid spike in sales within the first few hours. You'd expect that. But what you might *not* expect is that the very same email is still making sales over four weeks after it was sent!

This is because not everyone who will become a buyer is ready to buy *now*. But the email will be sitting there, in the inbox, and people will often fish it out when they're ready to buy. I can see from my tracking figures that this is undeniably true.

An email newsletter lets you gather marketing intelligence and do market research

By looking in your email software at which links your readers are clicking on most often in your emails, you can see which topics and products they're most interested in.

You can also run very simple surveys within the email, to ask a specific question, that can help you to understand your audience more fully.

You can then use that information to guide what you do. You can create more compelling articles, and more in-demand products and services that are easier to sell, based around the intelligence you now have on the things that interest your readers the most.

Summary: Reasons to have an email newsletter

1. You can reach almost everybody with email.

2. Email is proven to be effective.

3. Email is cheap.

4. Email addresses are easier to collect than postal addresses.

5. Email is easy to track.

6. An email newsletter lets you track your best customers and prospects, to focus your marketing on them.

7. An email newsletter lets you see exactly which products or services a particular person is interested in.

8. An email newsletter reaches people your other marketing emails don't reach.

9. Email newsletters can still make sales weeks or even months after they are sent.

10. An email newsletter lets you gather marketing intelligence and do market research.

CHAPTER 4

The power of a printed newsletter

Email is great for newsletters, but it's not perfect. Not everybody will open your emails. So how does print compare?

Printed newsletters are seen as publishing, not as marketing

Although we're doing marketing, we don't want to *look* as if we're doing marketing! We never want to come across as desperate.

Most people don't see a printed newsletter as a piece of sales or marketing material. Instead, they see printed material as a piece of publishing. And who does publishing? Experts. Trusted and credible people in their fields. Someone who is an authority. So we can sneak in under the radar, publishing valuable material for the reader while also doing some marketing.

(Just don't put any gratuitous adverts in the newsletter, especially from anyone other than yourself, or you'll ruin the illusion!)

Printed newsletters activate the reader's brain more than a screen

On a deeper psychological level, researchers have found that printed material lights up far more areas of a reader's brain than electronic communication. In particular, printed material causes far more of a reaction than digital information in the parts of the brain that deal with emotion.

Even in people who see themselves as rational and logical, we now know that the emotional parts of the brain are where buying decisions are typically made. So that's good news: a printed newsletter can cause lots of activity in the part of the brain that's directly responsible for buying.

If you're interested in finding out more, do a search online for the Millward Brown print psychology study PDF.

Printed newsletters make it easier to read longer articles

In general, an article in an email shouldn't be more than around 700 words, because that's about the most a reader can take in. By contrast, if you want to include longer pieces, it's easier to do that in print. Lots of people find it easier to consume large amounts of information in print than on a screen.

Printed newsletters stay around longer than email

Does your product or service have a long buying cycle? If the item is expensive, customers can take months to do their research and make up their mind. This long sales cycle is an opportunity in disguise—we can send a newsletter while the customer or prospect is deliberating, to keep giving them positive messages, and keep ourselves uppermost in their mind. Many of your competitors won't bother to do this.

A printed newsletter can linger on a kitchen table, desk, or coffee table for months. It's easy for a prospect or customer to keep it handy, for future reference.

Print is more long-lasting than email. If the customer isn't ready to buy yet, the printed newsletter could still be around long after the email has been deleted or been pushed down the inbox.

Printed newsletters give you more opportunities to catch the customer when they are in a buying mood

The Royal Mail in the UK conducted research showing that advertising mail is kept in a household on average for 17 days. This gives us more than two weeks for the newsletter to keep doing its job.

Printed newsletters are read by more people than just the recipient

As with magazines, printed newsletters are easily passed around, and on average more than one person reads a copy of a printed newsletter.

This has the added benefit of helping to increase your list. If somebody who hasn't heard of you stumbles across your newsletter and likes you, they might check out your business and end up becoming a customer. It's a useful sort of referral marketing, and comes at no extra cost.

Printed newsletters build brand recognition

Printed papers are tactile—you can touch them and feel them. A nice quality paper, with well-designed and well-printed graphics, can convey a sense of security and trust, and give the impression that you are a reputable, solid, real-world, professional company.

Printed newsletters are unusual and make you stand out

When was the last time you received a real handwritten letter? You're probably struggling to remember, because email and electronic communication are becoming the norm now. People don't receive as much physical material through their letterboxes today as they did 10 or 20 years ago, including marketing materials.

So by sending a physical printed newsletter, you can stand out, because not many other people are doing it.

Print has a higher perceived value than an email, due to scarcity

Anyone can send an email. There's nothing scarce about an email, and it's easy to do—even if that means it's often done badly. You probably have at least 20 times the number of companies sending you an email newsletter than you do a printed newsletter.

Print is perceived as hard to do, and something that only "proper" companies do. It conveys feelings of establishment and trust.

For these reasons, people subconsciously put a much higher value on print than they do on email.

An envelope with a printed newsletter can contain other things too

If you subscribe to a magazine, you'll know that when it arrives on your doormat there are often loose inserts from advertisers inside the envelope or cellophane-wrapped package. Sometimes there are even free books or other giveaways. You can do this too.

Alongside the newsletter in the envelope, you can include "Free Standing Inserts" (FSI)—leaflets for your own offers—or physical free samples to encourage your customers to try something new.

A printed newsletter acts as a welcome, expected, and non-threatening delivery mechanism for your other marketing.

Printed newsletters can be distributed in your place of business

If your business has physical premises, you can leave your newsletter in a prominent place for readers to take a copy. It's a simple, non-threatening way for them to connect with your business, especially if they are new prospects who aren't already your customers.

The printed newsletter can encourage the reader to visit your website, where you can also then capture their email address. This use of offline media driving to online media can be very powerful, and will help build your email list.

Printed newsletters bypass the email spam filter and the Gmail Promotions tab

Email can have problems with deliverability, meaning that your intended reader never even sees it. For example, your emails can get caught in the early spam filters that remove emails before they ever get to your customer's email account. Even then, your email could end up in the spam folder. If it avoids that fate, it could end up in the Gmail Promotions tab, meaning there's less chance of it being read than if it arrives in the reader's primary inbox. I talk about this in more detail, and ways to avoid it, in the bonus chapter that accompanies this book. (See the front of the book for details of how to get the bonus chapter.)

By contrast, printed newsletters don't have to dodge spam filters. They sometimes have to dodge gatekeepers such as secretaries or assistants, but since they're not overt hardcore sales promotions they stand a better chance of getting to the intended recipient than most types of mail. For the most part, though, you can expect that your printed newsletter will at least get noticed, even if it doesn't always get read, which can be a big win compared to email.

Some facts and figures on printed direct mail

Some people feel that digital, email, and social media are the only ways to market these days, and that nobody bothers with print any more. *Big mistake.*

You can reach different people in different ways by using a range of media. Typically, the more affluent a person is, the less likely they are to respond to digital communication, and the more likely they are to respond to print and direct mail.

In case I need to convince you of the need to incorporate a printed newsletter into your marketing mix, I've added this section to give you some useful information.

Here in the UK, the Royal Mail is obviously keen to tell us all about the virtues of direct mail—in our case printed newsletters—so they commissioned some research back in 2013-2015, which took 18 months to complete.

It's a few years ago, but the general ideas are still valid.

See https://www.marketreach.co.uk.

Here are some of the most important findings for us and our printed newsletters:

- In psychological experiments, people value something they can see *and touch* 24% more highly than something they can only see.

- 57% claim that receiving mail makes them feel more valued. Sending mail creates a more genuine two-way relationship between brands and consumers.

- 86% of people say they have connected with a business as a direct result of receiving direct mail.

- 87% were influenced to make online purchases as a result of receiving direct mail.

- Open rates are very high compared to email: 71% for a brochure from a company they have ordered from before; 69% for a letter containing a promotion or special offer; 60% for a letter about a product or service they don't yet have.

- 26.7% bought or ordered from direct mail in the last 12 months.

Summary: The power of a printed newsletter

1. Seen as publishing, not as marketing.

2. Activates the reader's brain more than a screen.

3. Makes it easier to read longer articles.

4. Stays around longer than email.

5. Gives you more opportunities to catch the customer when they are in a buying mood.

6. Can be read by more people than just the recipient.

7. Builds brand recognition.

8. Stands out by being unusual.

9. Has a higher perceived value than an email, due to scarcity.

10. Can contain other things in the envelope besides the newsletter.

11. Can be distributed in your place of business.

12. Bypass email spam filters and the Gmail Promotions tab.

CHAPTER 5

Should YOU have a newsletter?

By answering just a few simple questions, you can very easily determine whether a newsletter will suit *your* business. Here's what I look for when I'm advising a client.

What type of business do you have?

If you own one of the following types of business, it's most likely that a newsletter will work for you:

- A small or medium-sized business.
- A professional practice (for example, financial advisors, solicitors, or accountants).
- A health practice (such as a chiropractor's, spa, clinic, or veterinary surgery).
- A service business.
- A consultant, author, or speaker.
- An e-commerce internet retailer.

What features does your business have?

If your business has most of the following features, it's particularly likely that a newsletter will work for you:

- Your prospect or customer needs to trust you, and perceive you as a credible and knowledgeable authority.

- You have prospects or customers who will be ready to buy at some point, but they aren't ready to buy yet.

- Your sales cycle takes more than one month to complete, from the time the prospect thinks they might have a need to the time they close the sale with you, so you need to keep them actively engaged and nurture them.

- You have repeat customers that buy more than once, and you want to keep them coming back for more (increase your customer retention).

- You want to sell higher-priced and more profitable products to more of your customers.

- You would benefit from referrals and word of mouth, where your customers refer new customers to you.

- You are looking to sell or exit your business at some point in the future, and increasing the value of your customer base will increase the value of your business.

What list of people do you have?

In these days of GDPR and increased data protection regulations, you need to make sure that your readers have deliberately opted in to receive your newsletter.

(See the book *GDPR for Dummies*, published by Wiley, if you are based in, and/or market to, people in the UK or the European Union.)

The number of people you need on your list is very much dependent on the type of business you run and the average transaction size of your business. As a general guide, if you have at least 200 email addresses or postal addresses, it's worth doing a newsletter.

What are the economics of your business?

The economics of producing a newsletter also need to be checked, to make sure they stack up for you.

If your transactions tend to be high-priced, such as a solicitor who averages around £5,000 for a case, then an email newsletter or a printed newsletter should easily be profitable, and will more than pay for itself.

If your transactions are much lower priced—for example, you sell stationery and have an average transaction value of £10—it might be that an email newsletter is better suited to you.

Having said this, you could still send a printed newsletter to your *best* customers who spend the most, even if you don't think you can afford to send it to everyone.

A rational way to think about your investment in a newsletter

It's sometimes difficult to see far into the future about how the investment you are making in your customers today will pay off over the coming weeks, months, years, and even decades.

So let me give you a concrete way to think about it, based on two simple questions:

1. What is the average amount of profit you make every time you make a sale?

2. How many of these sales do you need to break even on your investment in a newsletter?

If you think in this way, the chances are you'll soon realise that you don't need to make too many new sales for your newsletter to break even and move into profit.

PART 2

THE STRATEGY

CHAPTER 6

Benefit-Based Newsletters™: giving value while showing your values

My philosophy for how to create a newsletter is such a core foundation of your success that I've given it a name: the **Benefit-Based Newsletter™**.

For your newsletter, and every article in it, the benefits go two ways. Primarily: how will it benefit the reader; and only secondarily: how will it benefit you?

This is where you can get a massive advantage over your competitors. Many companies simply think about how their marketing communications will benefit themselves, seeing how many half-baked promotions they can shove down their customers' throats before they give up and stop caring.

The art of a good newsletter is to *make* the reader care. As Theodore Roosevelt said: people don't care how much you know, until they know how much you care.

So in a Benefit-Based Newsletter™, you're putting the reader first. Not you: them.

This brings in two related concepts: value and values.

Value: For every single part of your newsletter, you need to be asking: will *my* reader value this? Don't just think about a generic person: really think about your own readers and what they're going to get from reading this particular piece. Will *they* value the article enough to keep reading it, and to keep reading further newsletters from you?

How can you bring additional value over and above what others might provide? This can be in the form of comment, analysis, or how to react to a piece of news. Sometimes the reader won't immediately understand the value of what you're presenting: you'll have to demonstrate the value to them and explain why the information is valuable to them.

Values: In every single part of your newsletter, you need to embed and entrench the values of yourself and your company, so that the article could only have come from you. It's got your fingerprints on it. Your DNA. That's why using generic articles simply isn't good enough: for your newsletter to be effective at creating a connection with the reader, the reader needs to know what *you* stand for, how *you* think, what *your* values are. How do you treat your customers? Why should the reader continue to do business with *you*?

Example: benefits, value, and values

Let's look at an example to bring all these parts together.

Imagine you're running an accountancy firm, and your business prepares tax returns for clients. There's been a change in the tax laws, and some of your clients will be affected. How would a Benefit-Based Newsletter™ handle this?

Benefit: First of all, would this news be of benefit to your clients if they knew about it? For those who are affected, yes. For those who aren't affected, no. The easiest way to handle this is to clearly state in the article headline, or near the start of the article, who it's aimed at.

Then each reader will either be motivated to continue reading, or they will know they can move on. Next, would this article be of benefit to you (as a marketer)? Yes, because it's showcasing your expertise and demonstrating that you know what you're talking about.

Value: Secondly, will the client *value* the news? If they're still reading this particular article, yes. "Thanks for telling me—you could save me a lot of money with this!" That's the first reaction that we're aiming for, and it will come simply from the news itself.

But how can we add more value on top of merely giving the news? How can we make the article more valuable, and provide more benefit? We can start to provide analysis and action steps. Here's an example. Obviously in the real world we'd need to check that all our claims are accurate and genuine.

Example extract from an article

"Assuming you don't want to pay more tax, our Senior Tax Partner, John, has identified three proactive steps that you can take, depending on the size of your company. He had great success with the similar tax change that came in three years ago, and he was able to move 98% of our clients to a more favourable situation.

We've reviewed these recommendations with the tax authority and the trade association, and confirmed that they are legal, ethical, and appropriate.

Here they are… (1… 2… 3…)

Your personal tax advisor will be calling you within the next week to tailor the perfect solution for you, or if you're particularly worried, feel free to call us at any time."

Values: Thirdly, can we show our unique values in this example article? The text above does that in a few different ways. We've introduced our Senior Tax Partner, John, and shown that he can get results. By saying that we've checked with the tax authority and the trade association, we've shown that we're not cowboys likely to get our clients into trouble. We even mentioned ethics, to make it clear. Then we said that we will tailor the perfect solution for you, implying that we treat our clients as individuals, rather than giving the same solution to everyone. We've also made ourselves look like we understand that people could be concerned, and made ourselves look approachable, by telling anyone feeling worried to call us. We've shown a lot of the values that make us special, if not unique, all within the space of a few lines.

So let's wrap up. In conclusion, you're aiming to provide an article that the reader will genuinely find valuable, while demonstrating your own values, beliefs, and approach.

Remember: newsletter benefits come from giving value while showing values.

Summary: The Benefit-Based Newsletter™

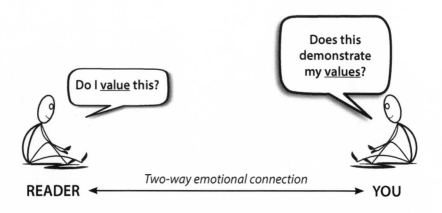

CHAPTER 7

The major strategic objectives of a newsletter

Now we're really going to go deep into the strategy behind making your newsletter a success.

This is the part that nobody else is going to tell you, so stick around!

The costs of advertising to get new customers is constantly increasing, especially online.

It is becoming absolutely vital that we *must* sell more to our existing customers, make those customers worth more to us, and increase our customer retention.

Yet how many business owners do you think really, truly understand what they're trying to *achieve* with a newsletter? Maybe on some superficial level, they think they're "doing marketing", but they don't have a true, deep understanding of what the objectives of their newsletter really are.

And if you don't know what you're trying to do, how can you do it?

To be effective, your newsletter needs to have a powerful strategy behind it. It can't just be the random musings of whatever you can conjure up at the last possible moment.

It needs to be *deliberately engineered* to squeeze every last possible advantage out of what you're doing.

Remember earlier, when I listed the benefits of having a newsletter? The following list of major strategic objectives is how you can practically go about very deliberately crafting your newsletter to get these benefits.

This might feel like a long list, but it is absolutely *crucial* to understand this.

A great newsletter must achieve these 32 major strategic objectives

1. **Affinity**: Showing that you are like your customers, and you have things in common with them.

2. **Ascension**: Moving your customers to buy more from you, at higher price points.

3. **Authority**: Proving your expertise and credibility; being naturally looked up to as the highest quality source of info, knowledge, products, and services in your market.

4. **Awareness**: Making sure customers remember that you exist and remember what you do.

5. **Branding**: Getting your name, logo, colours, and brand identity known without running expensive branding advertisements.

6. **Consumption**: Getting your newsletter opened and read is the vital first step to getting all the other benefits.

7. **Conversion**: Taking prospects who are not yet customers and nudging them into making their first purchase, so you acquire a new customer (often at very low cost).

8. **Demonstration**: Proving that you can help; demonstrating customers getting results, demonstrating customers referring others, and exhibiting the behaviour you want from good customers.

9. **Educational**: Telling the customer about the wider category of products and services that you sit within: for example, if you sell organic meat, we'd talk about the benefits of organic produce and organic methods in general.

10. **Engaging**: Providing interesting information that is appropriate to your customers and prospects (although not always directly related to your products and services).

11. **Entertaining**: Being interesting and never boring! Including fun content such as a crossword, word search, sudoku, cartoon, jokes, trivia, etc.

12. **Equity-building**: Strengthening customer relationships to make them a real asset when you want to get investment or sell your business.

13. **Follow-up**: Consistently staying in front of customers and prospects for a long period of time, especially after competitors have given up.

14. **Indoctrination**: Educating your customers with what you need them to know in order to make them great customers; hammering home your USP and your brand values.

15. **Likeability**: Showing you're not just a faceless corporation, and recognising that people do business with *people*; you want to be familiar and likeable—a friendly face!

16. **List-building**: Giving prospects who have been given or forwarded your newsletter an easy way to sign up to receive their own copies in future.

17. **Loyalty (exclusively)**: Making your customers buy from you, to the exclusion of your competitors (this is one step on from retention, where you could be one of many suppliers).

18. **Market intelligence**: Finding out what your customers want more of, and what they want next, by stimulating a two-way dialogue.

19. **Personality**: Revealing what you stand for: are you cheeky, playful, funny, serious, trustworthy?

20. **Positioning**: Standing for something special in the eyes of your customers; giving customers a clear view of who you and your team are, and what you can do for them.

21. **Referrals**: Getting current customers and readers to refer you to their friends, who could become new customers.

22. **Relationship**: Deepening the bond that your customers and prospects feel with you, and engineering a "pain of disconnection" so they don't want to go away or miss out.

23. **Relevant**: Showing that you are cutting edge, not stagnating, and are relevant to your industry and to your customers and prospects—the opposite of being irrelevant!

24. **Retention**: Keeping your customers for longer, for a higher customer lifetime value.

25. **Sales**: Creating short-term cash boosts, stimulating impulse purchases, and setting up longer-term sales success, without being seen to be salesy.

26. **Shareable**: Creating information worth passing on, that readers will want to share with others. This can mean either forwarding an email newsletter or giving a printed newsletter to someone, thus widening your reach.

27. **Social proof**: Showing that other customers are getting results and success from your products and services, by using case studies and testimonials.

28. **Timely**: Ensuring the newsletter contains up-to-date information, and giving a sense of urgency that the newsletter should be read immediately.

29. **Trustworthy**: Showing that you are a reliable and trustworthy business to be depended upon.

30. **Uniqueness**: Being clear about your USP, what makes you unique, and more valuable than your competitors in the eyes of your customers. Answering Dan Kennedy's question: "Why should I choose to do business with you versus any other choice open to me, including doing nothing?"

31. **Value-giving**: Providing info, offers, and entertainment that your specific reader finds *genuinely* valuable.

32. **Values-showing**: Showing the values, character, spirit, culture, standards, and ethos of you and your company.

Summary:
The 32 major strategic objectives of a newsletter

1.	Affinity	17.	Loyalty (exclusively)
2.	Ascension	18.	Market intelligence
3.	Authority	19.	Personality
4.	Awareness	20.	Positioning
5.	Branding	21.	Referrals
6.	Consumption	22.	Relationship
7.	Conversion	23.	Relevant
8.	Demonstration	24.	Retention
9.	Educational	25.	Sales
10.	Engaging	26.	Shareable
11.	Entertaining	27.	Social proof
12.	Equity-building	28.	Timely
13.	Follow-up	29.	Trustworthy
14.	Indoctrination	30.	Uniqueness
15.	Likeability	31.	Value-giving
16.	List-building	32.	Values-showing

CHAPTER 8

The various styles of newsletter

You'll need to decide what style of newsletter you're going to produce. We'll look at some of the options, and I'll give you my recommendation.

Article-based newsletters

This is the same concept as a magazine, with multiple articles, sections, quizzes, etc. Its super-strength is also its weakness: it can feel like easy reading, it's easy to skim, and the reader can read some sections in detail and skip other sections. There's a "something for everybody" feel to it.

You can use multiple authors, and either mention them by name or not. Having multiple authors can make it easier to put together this type of newsletter, since several people can work on it simultaneously, and it can be assembled at the end by an editor.

There's an element of safety in this approach. If one article isn't all that great, and misses the mark, there are other articles that can pick up the slack and be very valuable to the reader. If you have six articles, you have six chances to hit the mark!

For most people, I recommend you start with an article-based newsletter.

Personal-letter newsletters

This is like a letter from one friend to another. It has the feel of one author's voice (which is yours), even if you have it ghostwritten and don't write it yourself.

This style of newsletter has the danger of looking boring, or even *being* boring, but if you do it right then you can form a very strong relationship bond with the reader, to the point where they will look for your newsletter each month, and miss it if it doesn't arrive.

If you're the type of person who likes to write, you can sit down and imagine you're writing to a friend (because, really, you are!). If you prefer to talk, you can jot down a few reminder notes then set the voice recorder going on your phone, talk a stream of consciousness, then have it transcribed and cleaned up.

You can also get a journalist to interview you, and they can then ghostwrite the letter for you, in your voice. It can then be edited, proofread, and checked to make sure it hits all the major strategic objectives that you need. This interview method is often how I produce the personal introduction section of an article-based newsletter for my clients.

Although it's a personal letter, and is often made to look like one, you can still include images, sub-headings, and other things to keep the reader interested and break up the text.

Aggregation newsletters

These are a relative newcomer to the scene, and are really only done in email newsletters, not in print. The idea is that you send out a bunch of links to articles, blog posts, etc., that other people have written, that you think are interesting. The point of difference is that it's not your content, it's a series of links to other people's content.

The supposed benefit of this type of newsletter is to position yourself as a valued source of information, and as a sifting and sorting, discerning gatekeeper. Also, it can be quite quick to produce.

The negative is that, personally, I think it can come across as lazy: that you don't have anything to say for yourself. I think it positions you as a follower, not as a thought-leader. You also run the risk of sending people off to all the corners of the web, rather than concentrating on you and on your message.

The crucial key to making this style of newsletter work is the commentary that you add around the links. You need to give a few sentences to introduce each link, give your opinion on it, tell the reader why it's worth their time, and put your own spin on it.

You can achieve the benefits of showing you are a well-connected reference for good information, while still positioning yourself as a thought-leader, if you mix this kind of link recommendation with one of the other styles of newsletter mentioned above.

For these reasons I don't recommend that you do an aggregation newsletter; at least you should only do it as a second supplementary newsletter and not as your primary newsletter. If you have an article-based printed newsletter, you could consider doing an aggregation-style email as well.

Email newsletters: where should your articles go?

Email newsletters are usually a collection of short articles, often 500-800 words in length, because it's easier to read short chunks on a screen than it is to read a long personal letter.

The debate is then whether you include the entire article in the email, or whether you include a short summary and a link to the full article, which you then host on a blog.

In truth, you'll see great examples of both. This suggests that it might not matter too much which way you choose to do it.

The UK online stationery supplier Cult Pens has chosen to keep all its article text inside the monthly email newsletter, along with photos. The newsletter is very long, but very well done, and I enjoy reading it. Find them at https://www.cultpens.com.

The advantage of keeping everything within the email is that the reader stays fully within your world—once you have them clicking around and going onto the web, they are very easily distracted by pictures of cats and other whimsical diversions that don't help us to meet our goals.

The other approach, having short summaries of your articles and links that take people to your blog, first of all pre-supposes that you *have* a blog, that it looks good, and that it does all the things a blog should do.

It's a big job to get a blog set up, and it can take a lot of time to do it well. Unless you do lots of Search Engine Optimisation (SEO), don't expect many people to find your blog!

The benefit of sending out an email with lots of links is that you can see which links your readers are clicking, and gauge the popularity of the ideas, themes, products, and services you are putting forward.

Fortunately, if you take the route of putting the articles directly into your email, you can still include links within the articles, to items of interest, so you can get some of this benefit anyway by seeing which links get clicked on.

My recommendation is that you just include the full articles directly within your email. It's a lot easier, and I think it engages the reader more with the content as a whole, rather than encouraging a pick-and-choose mentality.

100% unique content versus off-the-shelf content

There are article libraries where you can buy pre-written articles ready to directly put into your newsletter or blog. You can even buy whole newsletters where most of the content is pre-written for you!

I really do *not* recommend this. There are several massive problems with using articles that are not unique to you.

Firstly, the articles are rarely great. They're often bland, obvious, unimaginative, and cranked out by the cheapest writers who may not understand your readers, at the lowest possible cost. They give no pleasure or information to the reader, so there is no reason for them to carry on reading your newsletter. The reader will simply not value them.

Secondly, an article written for a generic audience is not written for *your* audience. How can you achieve *your* objectives if you're just blasting readers with generic middle-of-the-road articles? *You* know *your* customers and *your* prospects, and you know what they want and how best to serve them.

Thirdly, using articles written for general use gives you no chance to inject those articles with your own vision and values, and your own ethos. You can't subtly educate or indoctrinate your readers into the things you need them to believe in order to buy.

Finally, if *you* can buy these articles, so can anyone else. Running the same articles as someone else is frankly embarrassing, and positions you firmly at the bottom of the pile.

———

My recommendation is that when you do a newsletter, you *must* use 100% unique content that is specifically written to come from *your* business and to go to *your* customers.

If a job is worth doing, it's worth doing well!

CHAPTER 9

The process for creating a newsletter

When I create a newsletter for a client, I have a very definite process. Let me show you how I do it, and you can do the same thing too.

It really breaks down into three phases: objectives, planning, and production.

The objectives phase

This phase should take you two or three hours. You might want to brainstorm it with a business partner or with your team, or at least get someone to review it when you've finished.

First, take a look at part one of this book, and see all the benefits a newsletter can give you, then choose the ones that feel most appropriate for you. There's no need to overthink this, it can be largely based on gut feel—you'll know what you want to concentrate on.

Second, take a look at part two of this book, at the 32 major strategic objectives, and choose the ones that feel most appropriate for you. Ideally you'll be able to achieve all 32, but it's good to choose the ones that you *really* want to make sure you accomplish.

Third, consider your customers. Think about their demographics (age, gender, geographic location, marital status) and psychographics (personality traits and values). This is the readership you're aiming at, and it's vital to understand them. Any writer or editor—whether that's you or someone else—will have to have a strong knowledge of your readership in order to produce a great newsletter.

On the next page I've given you an example of a reader description that I wrote for a client in the travel industry. As you can see, it doesn't have to be hugely detailed, but it gives enough information to know the sort of articles that would be appropriate, and those that wouldn't.

Fourth, if you were a client of mine, then during the course of our conversation I'd be listening to how you speak and developing ideas about your tone of voice and style of communication, so that we can make sure the newsletter matches it. You want to consider whether your tone is formal or informal; casual, friendly and colloquial or a little more stiff?

Useful questions to think about to help determine your tone of voice and style are:

- Would you write *do not* or *don't*?
- Would you write *kids* or *children*?
- Would you write *purchase* or *buy*?

The modern style of business writing is much more informal and simple than it would have been a few decades ago. This tends to make you appear more friendly, and also makes it easier to read and understand the contents of your newsletter. Go back and try to read a book from the Victorian era: it's tough going! We don't want that, or our readers will give up!

By the end of the objectives phase, you'll have worked out what you want to achieve, and the general direction you want to go in.

Example reader description for a travel newsletter

- Can be male or female.

- Mostly aged 60 to 79.

- All readers live in the UK.

- Usually spend a total of between £750 and £1,500 on booking their holiday (to include all the people travelling, not per person).

- Prefer to have the temperature on their holiday as between 20–25 degrees Celsius, and some people prefer hotter, between 26–30 degrees Celsius. Very few readers want anything colder or hotter than this.

- Want to know about good places to go on holiday, and what they can see and do when they get there.

- Travel for either one week or two weeks.

- Take a holiday of the following type (most popular first): sightseeing and culture, beach holiday, city break. Holidays can fall into more than one category, e.g. some days sightseeing and some days on the beach.

- Travel either on their own or with one other person (usually their spouse).

You only need to do the objectives phase once, although it's useful to revisit it every 6 to 12 months, just to make sure it's still correct.

The planning phase

Now you know your objectives, you can start to construct an editorial calendar. This doesn't have to be fancy, it just has to answer a few basic questions. Here are some examples:

- If you're sending a newsletter once a month, on what date will it be sent (for example, the first Monday of the month)?
- Which topics will appear in each issue?
- Can we tie a month to a theme, such as Christmas?
- What offers will you run for each of these months?
- What new products or services will you be launching, and when should you start to talk about them?

None of these decisions needs to be set in stone, and it can change, but it helps to get an overall plan, to shape the content.

You don't actually *need* an editorial calendar, if you find it difficult to plan ahead, but it can be helpful.

You should then prepare graphic designs, to show what the newsletter will look like. This stage can be fun!

For an email newsletter, this is then the point where you choose your subject line.

You can now choose your page count or size too. For an email newsletter, around 1,500 to 2,000 words is fine. For a printed newsletter, I'd start with four pages if you can. You need to use a multiple of four pages, so 4, 8, or 12 pages, because an A4-sized newsletter is printed by taking sheets of A3 paper and folding them in half, to produce four A4-sized pages.

You'll need to revisit your marketing calendar every few months, just to make sure it's still accurate and up to date.

Choosing your email subject line

My experiments, and those made by other marketers, have shown that the subject line that gets the most people to open your email newsletter is to use something that makes it clear this is the regular newsletter.

You can use a subject line named after your company, or you could give the newsletter itself a name. You could also summarise the contents of this issue. For example:

- Jones Solicitors Newsletter - October 2020
- Cult Pens Penorama: Review of the Year, Diaries, Discounts and Clearance Sale
- Your October Newsletter and Discount Code

Consider including the month and year, to make the newsletter look timely. It's important your readers can easily recognise that this is a newsletter, and not any other kind of marketing email.

The production phase

It's now time to move into the monthly cycle of producing a great newsletter.

Most of the skills I've outlined in this chapter are specialist disciplines in their own right. I couldn't possibly teach them all here without making this book huge. Graphic design, writing, editing, and proofreading are all areas that people spend years to learn and master.

The good news is that *you* don't have to be perfect in any of these areas, and you can bring in specialists for anything where you lack confidence. In particular, graphic design should not be left to amateurs!

There's some overlap between the stages I'll give you here, but this is the general process you need to follow:

1. **Monthly ideas**: Think of the general nature of the articles you want to include this month. Consult your editorial calendar to stay on-plan. If you can't think of specific details, you can ask writers to pitch ideas to you.

2. **Commissioning articles**: Commission articles from ghost-writers, journalists, and other authors. You want all your articles to be 100% customised to you, and written with your specific audience in mind. You're unlikely to want to write all the articles yourself: it can be time-consuming.

3. **Copy-editing**: Once you receive the articles from your writers, you'll need to refine them to make them consistently in tune with your personality and tone of voice. Check the facts and fix any grammatical issues. Potential legal grey areas (e.g. libel) should be addressed. The golden rule: if in doubt, leave it out!

4. **Layout**: Place the articles into the email template or newsletter template, and make them fit the space available.

5. **Images**: Place any images into the newsletter. These might be stock photos that you licence from an image library, or photos of your customers, team, yourself, or anything else you want to include. Check you have permission to use each image: some images are non-commercial use only.

6. **Linking**: Insert and check any hyperlinks for email, and also any discount codes (for email or print). This includes any tracking codes which we can use to directly trace activity and revenue back to *this* specific issue of the newsletter. This can involve you setting up necessary promotional codes in your sales systems.

7. **Proofreading**: Check the first full draft of the newsletter for accurate use of English, consistent spelling and

capitalisation, and any other mistakes or problems in the words, images, or layout. It's always best to get somebody else to do this, because at this point you're usually too close to your work, and you can't always spot the mistakes. The brain has a strange habit of seeing what you intended to write, not what you actually wrote!

8. **Specialist proofreading**: In some cases, a legal expert might need to proofread your newsletter. You could also get a subject matter expert to proofread it, or get a diversity proofreader or "sensitivity reader" if you are sending to some types of audience where you are not a specialist.

9. **Final check**: At this point you should just have a final look at everything and make sure that you're happy. If you were a client of mine, this is the point where I'd send everything to you for final approval. I like to prepare a checklist for each client and their email system, to make sure that each item (e.g. the subject line) has been correctly completed.

10. **Mailing list updating**: Update your email list or postal address list with the latest addresses, and make sure that any opted-out addresses are removed.

11. **Scheduling**: If you're producing an email newsletter, this is the time that you schedule it to be automatically sent at the appropriate date and time.

If you're producing a printed newsletter, you still have some more stages to go through:

12. **Send to mailing house**: Send a print-ready PDF to the mailing house. Here's a tip: use a fulfilment company that provides both the printing and the posting—it makes the world a lot simpler.

13. **Check printed proof**: Sometimes the printer might send a printed proof to approve, especially if you are a new client.

14. **Postage**: Physically send the printed newsletters to the readers.

15. **Returns handling**: Deal with any returned newsletters (e.g. "not known at this address"), and clean up the mailing list so we don't mail to them again. Your fulfilment company can often do this list-cleaning for you.

Legal issues and GDPR

There are a few legal considerations that we have to take into account with newsletters. These are, broadly:

- Data protection, privacy, opt-in, and opt-out.

- GDPR: General Data Protection Regulation, applicable in the EU (including the UK) but widely followed in the US. (See the book *GDPR for Dummies*, published by Wiley.)

- CAN-SPAM: Email data protection law in the US but followed worldwide, due to most Email Service Provider companies being based in the US. (CASL in Canada.)

- Copyright issues and clearances.

- Libel, defamation, inflammatory and obscene material.

- Regulations around competitions and giveaways (these are quite tightly regulated).

- If you're in the UK, make sure you're registered with the Information Commissioner's Office (ICO), at ico.org.uk.

I won't elaborate on these any further, because they are specialist areas that can get very detailed. They can change quite often too, so anything I write here might soon be out of date.

A professional proofreader or editor will have some awareness of these issues, and should be able to advise you of potentially troublesome areas.

You can seek special legal advice where needed, but for a simple life when it comes to legal issues: if in doubt, leave it out!

Summary: The process for creating a newsletter

1. Monthly ideas.
2. Article commissioning.
3. Copy-editing.
4. Layout.
5. Images.
6. Linking.
7. Proofreading.
8. Specialist proofreading.
9. Final check.
10. Mailing list updating.
11. Scheduling.

For a printed newsletter, the following extra steps are needed:

12. Send to mailing house.
13. Check printed proof.
14. Postage.
15. Returns handling.

CHAPTER 10

Be the conductor, not the orchestra: using freelancers

As you saw in the previous chapter on the process of creating a newsletter, there are lots of different skills that need to be brought together. The main skills are writing, editing, proofreading, and graphic design.

These are all specialist skills, and each can take many years of training, study, and practice in order to get anywhere near mastering. You probably don't have the time needed to get good at all these things. More to the point, you don't have time to waste—you want to get your newsletter sent out to customers as soon as possible!

The good news is that you don't have to master any of these skills yourself. If you're thinking like a business owner, you'll want to delegate the work and then check the final result.

My strong recommendation is that you hire experts to do the detailed work, and you just bring it all together. Act like the conductor, not the members of the orchestra.

When I was planning this book, I considered including detailed sections on writing, editing, and proofreading.

However, I soon realised that I could only ever cover these topics in an introductory way. After all, there are specialist societies, and even academic degree courses, on these topics! I could never hope to get you anywhere near a professional standard in all these skills in the space of just one book.

Instead, I can serve you better by teaching you the strategies and the things you need to know in order to *direct* the work, rather than to do all the work yourself. Then you can use outsourcing to rent the skills that you need.

Resources to help build your newsletter

There is often a big difference between working with amateurs and working with professionals, in all these fields. There's a lot more to all these skills than first meets the eye. I recommend you work with the best people you can afford, because you'll learn a lot from them, and you'll get professional results that can position you as the leading company in your field.

You can find most of the people you might need on a site called Upwork, at https://www.upwork.com. It's a site that allows you to post a job and a budget, and freelancers will apply to bid for the work.

I've had great results from Upwork, and the secret to making it work is to write a very good requirements brief, detailing exactly what you want. The better your brief, the better the work will be.

Freelancers are given a star rating by previous clients based on their previous work. I personally choose to pay more so that I can work with the best people with the highest ratings, but you don't always need to do that. You'll definitely find writers, designers, editors, and proofreaders on Upwork.

To help find wordsmiths, in the UK we have the Chartered Institute of Editing and Proofreading at https://www.ciep.uk, which offers courses and accreditation. Their standards are very high, and their members really know their stuff. They have a directory where you can find people that should fit your needs. You can also get proofreading done at https://www.wordy.com.

When you are writing and editing, Grammarly or ProWritingAid can be a very useful second set of eyes, but don't blindly accept their recommendations.

For graphic design, try 99designs at https://99designs.com.

If you're on a tight budget, you can find people at Fiverr that will help you with everything, and prices start from around $5. See https://www.fiverr.com.

If you've got a larger budget, and you want to work with publishing professionals, you can find vetted designers, editors, and proofreaders at https://reedsy.com.

Tips for successfully working with freelancers

One last thing: please, please, *pay your freelancers on time.* Many of them are self-employed, work very hard, and deserve to be paid as promptly as possible. Also, if you're happy with their work, please leave them a good review. It helps them to get more work, and they all tell me how much they appreciate it.

In the same way that freelancers get a star rating on platforms such as Upwork, so do clients like me when I'm hiring writers or other specialists. I'm very proud of the reputation I've built up with freelancers, by giving them clear guidance and instructions, paying promptly, and leaving reviews for them.

This excellent reputation means that when I post an assignment I get more freelancers applying to work with me, and I can usually secure the best freelancers quickly, because they know they will have a good experience working with me, get treated fairly, and get paid on time! I strongly recommend that you take the same approach.

When I hire freelancers, I expect their absolute best work, their care and attention to detail, and for them to keep to their commitments and deadlines. In return, I have to uphold my part of the bargain. This is what we'll look at next.

What freelancers need from you

When I was writing this chapter, I looked through all the five-star reviews that freelancers have left for me on Upwork, to see what led to our successful collaborations. To illustrate what freelancers need from you, in their own words, here are some extracts from these reviews. We'll then identify the common themes.

★★★★★ It's been a real pleasure working with Ian. The instructions were detailed, hence I knew exactly what I had to do. —*Lisa J*

★★★★★ Ian is great to work with. In particular, I appreciate his collaborative approach and clear guidelines. —*Bethany W*

★★★★★ Great client, very detailed and clear brief and excellent communication. —*Nick M*

★★★★★ Ian was great to work with, helpful, and informative about what he needed. —*Katherine K*

★★★★★ Ian was a pleasure to work with and would happily work with him again. He paid promptly upon the contract ending and his instructions were clear. —*Sally Anne H*

★★★★★ The job description was very clear and his instructions easy to follow. —*Mira D*

★★★★★ Very detailed about the work requirements, good communication and very responsive to messages. —*Emily P*

★★★★★ It was great to work with Ian again, communication is clear and deadlines reasonable. —*Fabio P*

★★★★★ Ian was a fantastic client to work with. He had an extremely clear outline of the content required, and open to answering questions. He even sent me a previous example of the newsletter so as to help substantiate what I needed to write. —*Alka Mariam J*

★★★★★ A great first experience for me of working with a client through Upwork. Professional and clear brief, with a reasonable deadline and pleasant interaction. I just hope that all Upwork clients and projects are like this! —*Pearl H*

★★★★★ Friendly client, good communication, clear and concise job description with fair pay and deadline. —*Miriam M*

★★★★★ Ian was fantastic to work with. His brief was clear, communication was prompt and friendly, and offered a fair fee.—*Bethany W*

★★★★★ Ian's task was straightforward, meticulously described and included very helpful examples and actionable tips. His communication was always prompt and polite.—*Goran P*

Based on this feedback, we can draw out some common themes from these comments. What freelancers need from you, to give you their best work:

- Clear and detailed instructions. Include a good description of your readers, as I mentioned in an earlier chapter.

- Clear and prompt communication when they ask questions (and the good freelancers will often ask questions to clarify the brief and make sure they're doing the right thing).

- Clear deadlines, which are also reasonable—I rarely give anyone less than a week to do their work, so that they can let their ideas brew in their mind before they start.

- A collaborative approach.

- Be pleasant and polite, and respectful of their time and skills.

- An example of a previous issue of your newsletter, so they can see your writing style and editorial voice.

- Fair pay. You can look at similar jobs to judge market rates.

- Prompt payment when work is completed. (I try to pay the same day as the work is completed, wherever possible.)

Let me handle the freelancers for you!

Do you want a one-stop-shop to get your newsletter "out the door" and making money for you? To apply for a Strategy Session to see if we could work together, visit:

www.NewsletterExpert.com/call

CHAPTER 11

Building your distribution list

If you've been in business for a reasonable length of time, you'll most likely have a list of customer email addresses and customer postal addresses. Under the GDPR regulations which are now in force, these people need to have opted in to receive marketing communications from you, otherwise you cannot legally contact them.

If you operate a business like a cafe or retail shop, where your customers just walk through the door, you might *not* have a list. If not, you really need to start gathering those names and putting the magical power of a newsletter to work for you.

For now, I'll assume that you've got a list of some sort, and the people on it have given you permission to contact them.

List-building is a big topic, worthy of a book or a course in its own right, and I won't cover it in its entirety here. You should be aware that it's possible to go into a lot of depth on list-building if you wish.

All I want to do in this chapter is to make you aware of some of the main concepts, and give you some ideas which are specific to newsletters, to help you get your newsletter to a wider audience.

Building a distribution list for any newsletter

- Make sure your newsletter tells people how they can sign up to receive future copies. If the newsletter is forwarded to someone, or handed to them by a friend, they need to know how to get onto your list.

- Whenever you are capturing someone's contact details, you must get permission to market to them, under the GDPR regulations. Don't do something bland, like a simple "Sign up to our newsletter"; give them a strong benefit-led reason to give permission, e.g. "Receive our newsletter and get exclusive special offers, discounts, and early-bird access to our hottest deals."

- Mention your newsletter in your social media. Let people know when you have a new issue out. Make it a big deal.

- Refer to your newsletter in your other marketing. "We had an article in the June edition of our newsletter that covers this exact topic. If you want a copy, here's what to do..."

- If you have a book, put a call-to-action for the reader to sign up to your newsletter prominently within the book. Bonus tip: put this right at the start of your book, then people using the Amazon "Look Inside" feature can see it, even if they don't buy your book!

Building a distribution list for email newsletters

- Inside the email, ask readers to forward the email newsletter to someone else if they've found articles useful, inspiring, or uplifting.

- In your email signature, include a link for people to sign up to your newsletter. As above, give them a strong benefit-led reason to do so.

- Have a prominent newsletter sign-up feature on your website and blog. You can offer a free exclusive item only available to people who sign up, such as an e-book or a special report that is valuable to your best prospects and customers. (This is often known as a lead magnet.)

- If you can see from your email tracking that a particular subscriber isn't reading your email newsletter, run a customer reactivation campaign. You've seen these before: it's those emails with the subject line, "Do you still want to hear from us?" There's an art and a science to doing these, which I won't go into here, but if you can offer something special to refresh a jaded subscriber and get them reading again, that's as good as getting a new subscriber.

Building a distribution list for printed newsletters

- Send a copy of your printed newsletter with every customer order that you send out.

- Put a copy of your newsletter in the bag with every purchase a customer makes in your shop or place of business.

- Leave your printed newsletters on your counter, reception desk, in your waiting room, and everywhere else they might be seen and picked up. Be sure to keep these places topped up with fresh copies. Make it clear that the reader can take one, free of charge.

- If you send correspondence for other reasons, such as promotional mailings, written quotations, or invoices, include a copy of your newsletter.

- In your newsletter, feature other businesses who do not compete directly with you, in a positive light. You can then see if they will distribute the newsletter to *their* mailing list, or make it available at their place of business, on the grounds that it will be good publicity for them too.

- Find a reason to get your customer's postal address, and make sure you also get permission to market to them. Run an offer where you send them a free book, or a free report, or some kind of free trial product or sample. Then, along with what you promised, you can also include a copy of the newsletter, and then keep those people on your distribution list for future issues.

- Ask the reader to pass the newsletter on when they are finished with it. You can present this as an environmental benefit: "Think of the environment: when you've read this newsletter, why not pass it on to someone else who would enjoy it!" Then, if you've done your job right, that person will see how they can also get on your list. Referral marketing at its most subtle!

- Share a link to a PDF version of your printed newsletter on your social media channels, every time you publish a new issue.

PART 3

THE ARTICLES

CHAPTER 12

Ideas for your articles

Now it's time to take a look at exactly what you can actually put in your newsletter, to interest your readers and to accomplish your major strategic objectives. With the ideas I'm giving you in this final part of the book, you'll never be short of something to write!

A golden opportunity

I'm really excited for you to read this section, because almost everyone thinks that their business is so boring that they can't possibly write anything that anyone would ever want to read! Fortunately, nothing could be further from the truth.

Right now, as business owners, we've got two big trends working in our favour, giving us a golden opportunity.

Firstly, the dire quality of most journalism today, caused in part by the expectation that it should be free, means that *we* can win attention by providing genuinely high-quality articles. We can be the source of real facts and real news. We can be a discerning sifter and sorter of information, giving our readers the best and most relevant information.

Secondly, many companies have foolishly shifted away from sending direct mail (that comes through your letterbox) and are now only sending email and doing online marketing. This means that people don't have much printed material landing on their doormat any more, so it's a bit of a novelty, and we can stand out and get noticed simply by sending something physical in the post.

Ironically, Google uses direct mail to sell its online advertising services, so what does that tell you: direct mail works!

Themes and tie-ins

An important concept in direct marketing is to enter the conversation that's already going on in your customer's head. This was laid down by Robert Collier, an advertising copywriter, almost a century ago. It means tapping into the themes that are already resonating with your reader. Their brain is already in that gear, and they'll be more receptive to your ideas.

This also has the advantage of making things easier for us, by doing some of our thinking for us!

For an email newsletter, you want to find something that the reader will still remember, and will still be relevant, a week after you send the email. For a printed newsletter, you want to find something that's going to have a shelf life of at least a month from when you send it out, which due to print deadlines means around five to eight weeks from the time it is written.

It can help to plan these themes and tie-ins in advance, using your yearly marketing calendar.

If you search Google for "Events in May", or "Celebrations in October", for example, you'll soon find plenty of inspiration. Make sure you're looking at UK dates rather than US dates (or vice versa, depending on where you live), since some celebrations, such as Mother's Day or Armed Forces Day, take place on different dates in different countries.

Monthly themes

You can theme the overall content of a newsletter based on the month it's going out. Here are some ideas (with UK dates):

Month	Ideas
January	New Year, New Year's resolutions, a new start. Goals, planning, what to accomplish for the year.
February	Valentine's Day. Pancake Day (can be in February or March).
March/April	Spring, and Easter: signs of renewal and new life in your area. Mother's Day. April Fool's Day.
May	Nothing major, so look for local events or minor celebrations that you can tie into what you do.
June	Father's Day.
July	Half-way point for the year. How are you getting on with your goals? American Independence Day.
August	Summer holidays, fun, no school, sunshine, relaxing.
September	Back to school. (This can mean education in its broader sense for your reader, not just literally school.)
October	Halloween.
November	Bonfire Night. Thanksgiving, although a US holiday, is starting to become more known in the UK thanks to Black Friday and its "bargain" sales offers, so you can talk about the theme of gratitude.
December	Christmas. A period of rest and relaxation, or busy excitement!

Other themes

These will be dependent on what you and your company values most, and what your customers and prospects value. If you're running a family firm with a commitment to family values, you can make use of family connections to give a theme to some of your editions. If you can't stretch these to be the theme for a whole edition of a newsletter, they could at least make one or two articles.

You might also consider themes around:

- Your birthday; your wedding anniversary (theme of commitment or love); your anniversary of company founding (theme of lasting service and reliability).

- Celebrity birthday, celebrity anniversary of death (e.g. 100 years since a particular artist, scientist, or author died).

- Anniversary of a major event or discovery—try to make it something happy and positive, and steer clear of wars or controversial events!

- A marketing day that somebody else has made up but actually exists: Letter Writing Month (April), Fountain Pen Day (first Friday in November), National Fish and Chip Day (first Friday in June). If you do a Google search for *weird national days* you'll find inspiration, including Compliment Day, National Spouses Day, Fun at Work Day, and World Nutella Day.

- A marketing day that *you* have made up yourself! Either serious or deliberately funny!

- News events—preferably not political, religious, or contentious.

- Celebration of your new product or service being launched.

- Moving office, moving house, opening a new location.

Be careful of tie-ins to sporting events or films

You might be tempted to build a theme around major sporting events or a major film release, but these can often have trademark and intellectual property problems, since companies often have to pay to do these kinds of marketing tie-ins.

My advice is to stick to something generic, so just mention football but not the FIFA World Cup™ itself, or just stay on safer ground and choose something else.

A quick way to get ideas for articles

A useful tip if you're struggling to think of what you could include in your newsletter is to grab a magazine (either within your category or outside it) or pick up a newspaper.

Then look at the articles and try to figure out the category of each article and its purpose for being there. Is it a how-to? Is it there to bond with the readers?

How can you take the idea or concept behind that article and turn it into something that's relevant to *your* readers?

Ask yourself:

- What topics are they covering?
- How are they covering them? What angles do they take?
- What sort of sections, features, and headlines do they have?
- What are they *not* covering, that you could either include or should avoid?

To read thousands of magazines online, including major titles, have a look at www.readly.com.

CHAPTER 13

How to grab your reader's attention with great headlines and more

For you to achieve most of your major strategic objectives, you need the reader to actually read some of your articles. So assuming that your articles aren't boring, let's look at some extra ways we can grab the reader's attention and get them to engage with us.

You need strong headlines

Marketing copywriters—people who write the text that goes into advertisements—say that "The headline is the ad for the ad". In our case, this means that the headline for one of your articles is trying to sell the reader on the idea that they should read the whole article.

So it follows that you must have strong headlines for your articles.

Interestingly, the only place where this doesn't seem to be true is the subject line of newsletter emails, where my tests have shown me that a simple subject line of "*Acme Company Newsletter - September 2020*" usually outperforms pretty much anything else. But then you could argue that this subject line *is* strong in the way that it needs to be: it shows this is a recurring email, that the reader is hopefully expecting, that's going to be useful and not just a marketing push to shove sales material down the reader's throat. As with anything though, it all depends on *your* particular audience.

You can use these headlines to make a table of contents on the front page of a printed newsletter, to encourage readers to open it up and get reading! In an email newsletter, you can have a section at the top named "What's in this issue?", which also uses these headlines.

Once you've identified a strong headline, the rest of the article starts to write itself, because you've got a strong idea to run with. I'm not going to go into the art and science of great headlines, because that's a whole book or course in itself, but I want to show you some headlines to give you some ideas.

You might argue that some of these headlines are clickbait, and to some extent I'd agree. Of course, you've got to know your audience and tailor your writing to them. But there's a reason clickbait is used online: it's very effective. It taps into deep-seated psychological desires that make us find things interesting, and make the reader think: "I've got to find out more."

A quick tip if you're doing clickbait: it's well known by the people who write and publish those articles that lists with an odd number of items do better than lists with an even number of items. Strange but true. That's why you don't usually see articles with eight tips, they either have seven or nine! (Top tens are the only thing that seems to escape the clutches of this one.)

Questions are also useful in headlines because they create curiosity and draw the reader in, sometimes to see whether the answer they have in their head is the same answer that you're going to give, and sometimes because they have no idea of the answer and want to find out.

With our headlines, we're usually aiming to be closer in style to popular magazines than to a broadsheet newspaper, so looking at magazines can also help give you some thoughts on headlines and how to tackle a subject.

Most headlines work on one, or both, of two things: curiosity and a promise of information. You can see this in the following list of headline suggestions.

Article headline ideas

1. 9 ways to save time when xxx
2. A crash course in xxx
3. A tried and tested way to xxx
4. How could xxx ever have happened?
5. Can we talk openly about xxx?
6. The 7 secrets to xxx
7. Planning xxx on a budget
8. Should you switch to xxx?
9. 5 deadly xxx mistakes you might be making
10. 9 Tips to simplify xxx
11. Tips to teach xxx about yyy
12. Don't let fears of xxx paralyse you
13. 9 money-saving tips for xxx
14. A new way to do xxx without yyy
15. How to stop xxx
16. What are your hopes for xxx?
17. 11-point checklist: xxx
18. How to survive xxx
19. 7 proven ways to xxx
20. 15 things you didn't know about xxx

21. What we learned from xxx

22. 7 creative ways to xxx

23. Tips for a great xxx

24. Are you going to xxx?

25. Why everything you know about xxx is wrong

26. The beginner's guide to xxx

27. Can you really xxx ?

28. Here's 5 things to put you in a good mood

29. How I did xxx in just 7 days

30. 9 signs you might be xxx

31. 5 great reasons to xxx

32. 7 reasons why having an excellent xxx is not enough

33. To xxx or not to xxx?

34. What's it like to have xxx?

35. How to get rid of xxx once and for all

36. 10 xxx for under £100

37. 11 xxx myths exposed

38. 5 big mistakes with xxx that you can easily avoid

39. When is the right time to xxx

40. What we found by xxx

41. Can you really xxx just by yyy?

42. Top 10 tactics the professionals use to xxx

43. Why we no longer xxx

44. The most common mistakes we see with xxx

45. Where will xxx be 6 months from now?

46. 17 reasons you should xxx

47. The anatomy of xxx

48. 7 tips for a better xxx

49. What you've never been told about xxx

50. How to get started with xxx

51. The easy way to xxx

52. Proof that xxx is better than yyy

53. The day I nearly xxx

54. I wish I'd known about xxx

55. What on earth is xxx?

56. Have you ever xxx?

57. What everyone needs to know about xxx

58. Why I don't xxx

59. 7 things I like about xxx

60. What will be the hottest xxx in 2025?

61. The greatest xxx tips of all time

62. How to do xxx like a pro

63. The perfect xxx

64. 5 alternatives to xxx

65. The truth behind xxx

66. These xxx were the godfathers of modern yyy

67. Get ready for (Spring/Summer/Autumn/Winter)

Other ways to grab your reader's attention

When a reader is skimming your newsletter, they'll see your headlines and decide whether to slow down and read in more detail. But there are actually far more ways we can grab the reader's attention than just the main headline.

What we're really trying to do here is set up what copywriters call a "dual readership path", where path one sees the reader skimming to get a good idea of the content, and path two sees the reader slowing down to read the full article. If you do this correctly, even if a reader skims the newsletter you'll still have accomplished some of your major strategic objectives.

Here are things we can use to grab the attention of a reader who's skimming your newsletter:

- Headlines
- Sub-headings
- Pull-quotes
- Image captions
- The PS at the end of a personal introduction or personal piece

Sub-headings break up the article, so it doesn't feel as long and heavy. We can make the sub-headings intriguing too, grabbing the reader's attention by getting them to pose a question or set up something in the reader's mind that demands an answer, forcing them to carry on reading.

A pull-quote is a small, eye-catching short sentence that helps to draw the reader in. This is an example of a pull-quote.

Pull-quotes are easier done in print, but they can be done in email too. You'll have seen pull-quotes used in magazines, and increasingly they are used in books too. They're a small, eye-catching, interesting, intriguing, or enticing few words taken from the main article and reprinted in large text somewhere within the article as a quotation. They really function in a similar way to a sub-heading, to guide the reader and illustrate key points, but can be a bit longer, and give you more layout options when a full sentence wouldn't really work as a sub-heading.

Image captions capture the reader's interest. The human eye is drawn to images, and very often a reader who is skimming your newsletter will read an image caption to get a sense of the article and what it's all about. So when you have an image, it's often best to have a caption that includes a piece of information you really want the reader to know.

The PS, short for postscript, comes from the days when we used to write letters. (I still do, and the art of letter writing seems to be making a bit of a comeback in the trendy art and craft community.) The basic idea is that after you sign off, you include a PS that reiterates an important point that you want the reader to remember, or a specific action that you want them to take. Use a nice, soft call-to-action, nothing giving a hard sell—remember, you're a publisher!

So at the end of your personal introduction section, you can sign off like this:

All the best,
Ian Howlett, founder of Newsletter Expert.

PS: Don't forget to get a quote and enter our competition to win a £50 Amazon voucher—it closes on Friday at 5 p.m.!

CHAPTER 14

Captivating Categories of Content™

It's important that you give your readers a balanced mix of content. The temptation is to include only information about what you actually do, and nothing else. This can be very boring for the reader, who won't stay reading for long! Also, if you're a dentist, you can't keep showing horrific photos of diseased mouths for too long, and if you do something that's fundamentally hard to make interesting, you can't talk about it directly for too long without sending people to sleep. For some businesses, such as a funeral director, it's hard to talk about what you do for too long without giving people the creeps!

So how do we get around this problem? We simply use ideas from all of the Captivating Categories of Content™. Notice that all the types of content work together, like an orchestra or the parts of an engine, with no one theme dominating.

This framework is incredibly powerful, because it makes sure that you include content from almost *all* of these categories in *every* newsletter. Each category has its own place and its own ways of meeting your strategic objectives.

In fact, no more than 50% of the content in your newsletter should be about what you actually do, or you won't achieve all the strategic objectives of your newsletter.

An individual article can focus on just one of these categories of content, or it can blend these different categories together.

Everything in your newsletter will fall into one of these overall categories. The important thing isn't the name I've given to these categories, or whether we split hairs about exactly what goes into each category, because there's some overlap. Rather, it's important that you notice the *function* that each of these pieces of content is performing, what it's aiming to do, and which strategic objectives it's intended to meet.

What-you-do content

This is information that is directly relevant to what it is that you actually do.

For example, if you're a solicitor, this will be information about the parts of the law that you specialise in. If you're in insurance, this will be about the specific types of insurance that you offer. It's essential to include some of this, but not too much!

Category content

This is information about your category—in other words, your industry—and how people ultimately use your product or service. It's information that addresses *why* people buy what you sell, and what they do with it, to stimulate more use of it.

For example, in travel insurance, this is where you write about holidays, destinations, city breaks, beaches, and travel tips—that's *why* the customer is buying the travel insurance, and that's what they're really interested in.

Another example of a category content strategy is the Michelin tyre company. They realised they would sell more tyres if people drove their cars more often and wore down the tyres, so in 1900 they published a guide to the best restaurants to drive to, giving people a reason to use their cars. This strategy proved so successful that the guide is still published today.

What-they-like content

This is information that isn't specifically about what you do, or your industry or category, but still has relevance and interest to the reader because it talks about things they like to read about.

Depending on your audience, this could include personal development, mindfulness, wellness, general consumer news, or anything else that isn't directly about your topic but will still be appreciated by your customers and prospects. You are bringing valuable information to the reader here, and building your reputation as a reliable source. You need to understand your customers well to get this right.

Relationship content and the personal piece

This is information that absolutely isn't about *what* you do, but talks about *who you are*, shows your values, and shows you and your team as genuine human beings.

It can be like a personal letter written to a friend. You don't have to share every last detail, but people want to know who you and your team are and what you stand for.

It's why soap operas are so popular: it's more about the characters themselves than it is about the plot. Never overlook this type of content: **it's essential!**

The single most important thing in your newsletter is the personal piece: a personal introduction from the face of the business, for example the founder, managing director, or CEO—that's probably you! Don't worry, it can be ghostwritten, where someone has a chat with you and then writes the article, so you don't have to do it yourself if you don't feel comfortable.

Community-building content

This is information that somehow references or involves your customers, or the people in the area where you live or work, to help build a sense of community around you.

This can include: welcoming new customers by using their name (if they have agreed to be mentioned); customer case studies, spotlights, and testimonials to highlight your success; Q&A with customers; interesting photos of readers; thanking people who referred new customers to you.

You can also include calendars for what's coming up in your business, your industry, and the wider world; reports on your charity work and community work; competitions and contests; readers' letters, emails, tweets, etc. Tell them how to contact you if they want their words to be considered for publication.

Sales content

This covers everything that's gently trying to make a sale.

Use this sparingly. No more than 10% of your newsletter should be sales content. Too much and you'll lose your positioning as being a publisher, and you'll appear as just another seller. Include details of sales, discounts, special offers, free trials, new product launches, etc.

Fun content

A quiz, word search, crossword, sudoku, jokes, cartoons, inspirational quotes, facts, and the kind of little fillers you'd see in *Reader's Digest* or something similar. This can be a big reason why people open your newsletter, so don't overlook it!

Teaser content

This is all about getting people curious, hungry for more, and making sure they keep reading the newsletter.

What's coming up in next month's issue? What did they miss in the last issue?

This is where you build buzz and hype around what's coming up in your business, and in the industry in general. What is there that "I can't say much about that yet", to add an air of mystique and intrigue? End on a cliffhanger!

Response content

The ultimate objective of your newsletter is to get readers to respond to you, which will then lead to more sales.

So even when we're not directly selling, we want to condition readers to get into the *habit* of responding to us. We do this with response content.

Asking your readers for their comments, views, and feedback are all examples of response content. You might ask them to post pictures linked to your social media, or to use your hashtags. Response content is anything that gets the reader into the habit of responding to you and engaging with you in some way.

Often, you can tag response content onto the end of another article, with phrases like "Email me to let me know what you think about this", "Just reply to this email to let me know your thoughts", or linking at the end of an article to a survey that you're running on that topic.

Referral content

This is the content deliberately designed to stimulate referrals and word-of-mouth marketing.

The intention is that your existing readers and customers can pass on your newsletter to someone who hasn't yet heard of you, but who could be a good customer for you. They can pass it on either by giving them a copy of your printed newsletter, or by forwarding your email newsletter. This helps to grow your customer base at no cost to you.

There are two parts to getting referral content right:

1. Encouraging the original reader to share your newsletter or its contents with someone they know. You could add something like "Do you know someone who should be getting this newsletter? Forward it on to them, so they don't miss out."

2. Getting the new reader who has received the newsletter to sign up to your list, so they can receive your newsletter every month. One way to do this is to include something like: "If you were forwarded this newsletter, click here for your free subscription."

Referral content can also include sales offers deliberately designed to stimulate referrals to get new customers, such as "Refer a friend: when they sign up as a customer you'll both receive a £20 gift card."

Structural content

This is the framework that holds everything together.

It includes your masthead at the top, logos for awards and professional memberships, certifications, a short table of contents, a footer with unsubscribe info and contact information, and links to where else customers can find you, such as your website, blog, social media channels, YouTube, books, podcast, etc.

A lot of this structural content is done as part of a professional design, and doesn't change much from month to month.

A more detailed look at some of these categories

In the next few chapters we'll take a look in more detail at some of these content categories, with plenty of examples and ideas.

How this same formula works in podcasting

To close this chapter, I want you to understand that this is *all* tried-and-tested material that has worked for *centuries* in all kinds of printed publications, then on radio, television, and today on podcasts and YouTube. It's timeless. Let me give you an example.

Podcasts are the flavour of the month at the moment with a lot of marketers. These folks who often think they're blazing a trail into the future, laying new paths that have never been trodden before, will often follow a formulaic structure for their shows that includes many of the Captivating Categories of Content™.

The table on the next page shows how a typical podcast will run, integrating these types of content.

It's harder to do Fun content such as a quiz or sudoku on an audio recording, so it tends to be mixed throughout the rest of the show, especially if the podcaster has a naturally funny and chatty personality. That's the equivalent of the tone of voice that we aim for in a newsletter.

Notice how there's a rhythm to what the podcasters do: a regularity, a consistency, a "same every month" feel. That's what we're doing with a newsletter too.

Item	Content category
Theme tune and pre-recorded welcome that's the same every time.	*Structural content.*
The pre-recorded welcome often mentions a long-standing free trial offer or website.	*Sales content.*
The pre-recorded welcome often mentions how to subscribe to the podcast.	*Referral content to grab a first-time listener.*
Personal monologue about what the podcaster did this week outside of work.	*Relationship content, the personal piece, What-they-like content.*
Personal monologue about the podcaster's progress with their own work; announcements.	*What-you-do content.*
Request for the listener to leave a review of the podcast, send in their comments, or to comment on social media.	*Response content.*
Ask the listener to share the podcast.	*Referral content.*
Industry news and news on the topic.	*Category content.*
Some kind of Q&A discussing listeners' questions that they have sent in.	*Community-building content and What-you-do content.*
A thank you to new subscribers (whose names are read out) who have signed up to donate a couple of pounds a month (via Patreon) to support the podcast.	*Community-building content with social proof.*
An interview with a guest who can shed light on a topic, and is probably promoting a book or some other product—a time-honoured tradition from TV chat shows!	*What-you-do content, Category content, Sales content.*
Question of the week (such as: "What are *your* top tips for productivity?"), and an invitation to listeners to give their response, either by email, tweet, or as a comment on a blog.	*Community-building content, Response content.*
What's coming up on the next show.	*Teaser content.*
Theme tune and pre-recorded end-of-show message, repeating an offer.	*Structural content, Sales content.*

Summary: The Captivating Categories of Content™

1. What-you-do content.
2. Category content.
3. What-they-like content.
4. Relationship content and the personal piece.
5. Community-building content.
6. Sales content.
7. Fun content.
8. Teaser content.
9. Response content.
10. Referral content.
11. Structural content.

CHAPTER 15

What-you-do content and Category content

I'm going to group What-you-do content and Category content together in this chapter because, depending on what you sell, the line between them can be a bit blurry.

We're looking at three things here:

- **Your company's products and services**: The products and services that your company specifically offers.
- **Your category or industry**: The wider world of products, services, and experiences in your area.
- **Ancillary or complementary products**: Anything else that your product needs in order to function, or is often paired with your product.

Let's look at an example. I like fountain pens, so let's imagine you're a specialist fountain pen retailer. Yes, they do still exist! How would What-you-do content and Category content look for you in this case?

Your company's products and services: The specific fountain pens, ink, and paper that you sell, and the repairs and servicing that *you* offer; new releases and upcoming products that you will be stocking.

Your category or industry: The wider world of stationery; fountain pens in general, both historic and modern; repairs and servicing in general; pen manufacturers and what they're getting up to; comments from other leaders and experts in the field.

Ancillary or complementary products: Anything that goes with a pen: ink, paper, notebooks, pencil cases, books on the topic, courses, societies that customers can join, such as the Writing Equipment Society (yes, that exists too!).

Timeframes: three bites of the cherry!

I'm about to give you lots of specific ideas. You'll see that for a lot of these ideas, there are three timeframes you can use when you're writing:

- Something will be happening in the future.
- Something is happening now.
- Something has happened and I'm reporting on it.

So you can write about the same occurrence multiple times, in different issues of your newsletter, as that thing moves through these timeframes.

Ideas for What-you-do content and Category content

1. A detailed look at a product or service that you offer.
2. Q&A with you, your team, or industry experts.
3. Upcoming industry events that your readers will want to know about.
4. News about your company.
5. Mentioning a book, magazine, or other piece of media where you are mentioned, featured, or interviewed.

6. Your company history—be careful, because this can be boring, but if you've been running for many decades you can tie it to a fascinating "What life used to be like" piece.

7. Report on an industry event, seminar, workshop, or trade show where you spoke, exhibited, or were a sponsor.

8. Links to relevant blogs, videos, articles, books, and publications that relate to what you do—either produced by you or by someone else in the industry who is not a direct competitor.

9. Run a poll or survey that will help you make a decision in your business, such as what product to develop next, or what types of things are popular with readers.

10. Give the exact results of a previous poll or survey. Can you turn this into some kind of bigger marketing piece, like a special report or white paper with a topic like "What we learned from surveying 500 doctors"?

11. Use the results of a survey to figure out where users need help, then write an article that provides that help (and shows which of your products and services can help them more).

12. Positive environmental progress you are making, e.g. more recycling, using less packaging.

13. Articles you have appeared in or have written for other people's magazines, newspapers, websites, guest blogs, podcasts, etc.

14. Buyer's guide, shopper's guide, round-up.

15. How to shop for your category of product or service—what to look for, what traps to avoid.

16. A gift guide: at Christmas, what sorts of things should readers buy from you for their relatives?

17. Make predictions for the future of your industry. People love predictions, and they think that only experts can make them, so it positions you as an expert. Even if a prediction later turns out to be wrong, people usually forget it anyway, or let you off the hook, because everyone knows you can't really predict the future. Look at stock market "experts"—their predictions are often wide of the mark, but it doesn't seem to do them any harm.

18. How-to articles.

19. Experiences people have had that somehow relate to your product or service.

20. A walk-through of one of your products or services.

21. Interviews with industry leaders, experts, and other people in your industry.

22. Notifying readers of where you will be speaking or exhibiting—shows your expertise and builds authority.

23. Awards and competitions you are entering: just the act of entering makes people think you're good, because if you weren't, why would you even enter?

24. Awards that you need your readers to nominate you for.

25. Awards you have won.

26. Holiday closures for Christmas, bank holidays, Easter, etc. This might include telling people about longer delivery times over the holidays, last order dates, etc.

27. Updated opening hours.

28. Calendar of events. This can include items for your company, your category or industry, and the country as a whole (e.g. a royal wedding or a major football final).

29. "Save the date" to specifically draw attention to your upcoming events, webinars, sales, etc. Words like "Save

the date" or "Dates for your diary" look like editorial content to the reader, even though they are often really there to promote things for you.

30. Best-practice updates or discussions.

31. Top 10 articles (often called listicles by trendy people).

32. Regular columns or columnists, themed to the topics of your business.

33. A roundup of what's currently in the market, such as "20 pens for under £20".

34. Report on an industry event that you attended.

35. Behind-the-scenes: a look at how you do what you do.

36. An infographic, either created by you, or shared from someone else (with their permission, although infographics are often designed to be shared, so getting permission shouldn't be hard).

37. Statistics relating to your industry, product, or service, that prove a point or show that you're on-trend.

38. Adding extra dates, classes, or somehow expanding a programme you're already running.

39. Reviews of products, books, films, etc. related to your industry.

40. Editorial opinion: what do you think about a certain topic or issue in your industry?

41. Educational guides to industry topics: these can be beginner, intermediate, or advanced. You can point readers to courses or other products and services you offer if they want to continue their learning further, or if they want to hire you to actually do the thing you're talking about for them.

42. A summary of posts on your blog this month, to drive readers to those posts.

43. Notice of improved delivery times.

44. Information on new partners, suppliers, and distributors that you are working with.

45. Consumer protection: warnings of cons, scams, and sharp practice in your industry (be careful of this from a legal perspective—don't name names).

46. Dos and Don'ts.

47. Classic reprints: use it sparingly, but if an article has been particularly popular or useful, you can reprint it, either as-is or preferably updated (perhaps with the feedback you received, or stories of how the article helped people) so that it looks like you're offering something new.

48. Product maintenance and servicing advice.

49. New benefits that a customer will get from working with you.

50. Tips directly relevant to your products, services, and the problems you solve.

51. Tackle your problems head-on: if lots of customers are experiencing a particular problem or issue, tell them how you're dealing with it, and what they can expect.

52. Market analysis, which could include facts, figures, statistics, trends, etc.

53. How your product is made or produced, e.g. an organic farm shop talking about how their meat is reared to high welfare standards, with demonstrations and proof.

54. Information on stock levels ("this pen has been out of stock for months, but we're getting a new delivery at the end of September").

55. Your unique selling proposition (USP), how you're bringing it to life for customers, and what it means to them.

56. Frequently asked questions (FAQ) that you can answer.

57. Apps, software, websites, or tools that are helpful in your work.

58. An agony-aunt style advice column.

59. Industry news.

60. Updates to policies, e.g. your privacy policy.

61. A review of your company year, with interesting facts, e.g. how many lives did you improve, or (more frivolously) how many cups of tea did your people drink during the year?

62. Little-known uses for your product or service.

63. Dedication to your cause or brand promise, such as an organic cafe talking about the organic movement in general.

64. Resource of the month: some kind of useful website, technique, template, or other small item the reader will find useful.

65. How your product or service got someone out of trouble! (Useful for insurance, legal, rescue, and recovery sorts of businesses.)

66. How a customer avoided a problem because of the quality of your product or service (for example, you're an accountant and your client got investigated by the tax authorities, but thanks to your great work your client was found to be squeaky-clean).

67. Pick of the month: the best (something) we've seen this month. This could be the best uses of your products, the best innovative or creative ideas in your category, etc.

68. Your guarantees, and how you reduce risk for customers.

69. Link to a demo video of one of your products or services.

70. Positive media coverage that your company, products, or people have received.

71. Remind the reader of the existing benefits that customers get from working with you. Make them aware, because sometimes customers don't actually use (or know about) everything they're entitled to from you as a result of packages they have bought from you.

72. Tip of the month.

73. Ask your customer service people what types of questions they often get, and then write articles that address those questions and the deeper issues they raise.

74. A new location or premises you are opening.

75. Famous people or celebrities that use or endorse you (ask their permission first).

76. Company milestones and anniversaries.

77. Discussion of a new advertising campaign you are running, and why. What are you hoping to achieve? What do you want someone to know or think about you after they've seen the ads? This is an advanced strategy, because it lets you repeat a key advertising point while seeming like a trusted impartial commentator and not an advertiser (because you're publishing, not selling, right!).

78. A list of things for your reader to do this month, related to your type of business and the things you talk about. For example, in a gardening newsletter you'd give a list of what to plant this month, what to dig up this month, and what to do to prepare your soil this month.

CHAPTER 16

Relationship content and the personal piece

The main idea with Relationship content is that people buy from people, so you want to humanise your company and let people feel they are doing business with a friend.

Relationship content moves people along the "know, like, trust" spectrum: first they get to know you a little, so they start to like you. Once they start to like you, they start to trust you. Each issue of the newsletter builds on this, deepening the knowing, the liking, and the trusting.

Relationship content is often overlooked by people when creating a newsletter. It feels a bit soft and wishy-washy, and your instinct might be to think, "Who's going to care about any of this?" But not including some Relationship content is a huge mistake that will seriously weaken the effectiveness of your newsletter. Let other people's mistake here be your opportunity!

The key point is that we're trying to achieve a **soap opera feel**, with a cast of characters that readers will become familiar with, and want to keep up with what they're doing and what's going on in their lives. A soap opera—or "continuing drama" if you want to be upmarket—does a great job of getting viewers to come back time after time. They use cliffhangers, unresolved intrigue, and all manner of tricks. It really is a great metaphor for what we're doing in a newsletter with our Relationship content.

The huge importance of the personal piece

The personal piece is the secret key ingredient in most super-effective newsletters. It's the secret sauce, and you leave it out at your peril.

If you liken it to a newspaper or a magazine, the personal piece is broadly similar to the editor's introduction, an editorial, a comment piece, an opinion piece, an op-ed piece, or a leader column. It has the feel of a friendly one-to-one chat with someone you know.

Church magazines or parish magazines seem to do quite well at the personal piece: maybe vicars and priests have a natural way of connecting with their flock that we can try and emulate.

In a printed newspaper, it's often good to have the personal piece as the first item on the front page. In an email newsletter, I like to put the personal piece before the articles. Some emails have the personal piece right at the bottom of the newsletter, like it's the least important thing. Wrong: it's actually the *most* important thing, so put it near the top or people will miss it if they stop reading.

What goes into the personal piece?

The easiest thing to include is simply to introduce the articles in this issue of the newsletter, and perhaps add a bit of commentary. Why did you choose these specific topics? What's the context? Magazine editors do a good job with this, so if you want to see some good examples, see the letter from the editor that appears at the start of most magazines.

However, introducing the articles is only a starting point, and it's optional. You can build a more powerful connection with the reader by including personal things. What's going on in your life? How's your month been? Who have you met? What have you seen? What are you hoping to do? You don't need to come across like a superhero here—it can sometimes be off-putting if the author seems too perfect. We are all human, we all make mistakes, and we are made to seem more human by our mistakes. So you can share little foibles, goofs, and the odd faux-pas. Obviously an accountant who admits to committing a huge fraud or embezzling funds isn't going to be received too well, so use good judgement!

A common approach is to use some kind of event or observation that you've made in order to make a wider point, or to draw a wider lesson. This is the territory of religious preachers (again), Jesus, stand-up comedians, and motivational speakers. These are all interesting types of people to study and to get ideas from. The classic American success speakers of the past—Jim Rohn, Zig Ziglar, Napoleon Hill—all do this a lot: taking a story and weaving a parable with a deeper meaning and a point they want to teach. Great sales people, marketing people, and copywriters all use a lot of stories in their selling.

A lot of these personal pieces end up being a short personal development article. That's fine, because this is all about relationship and personality.

Formula for writing the personal piece

There's quite a simple formula you can use to get you started when you're writing your personal piece.

I call it **Situation—Key Point—Relevance**. Each part of the formula only needs to be a sentence or two. There's no need to go into too much detail or it might start to drag. There are other ways to do it, but this formula will get you started.

THE SITUATION

- **Teaser opening**: A quick line to get things going and build curiosity. For example, "I noticed something odd the other day.", or "It's been a crazy week—let me tell you about it!"

- **An event, story, or fact**: mention something that's happened. It might be a fact, or it might be a little story.

- **Another event, story, or fact**: optionally, mention something else that's happened or that you've seen that's in some way connected. This can flesh out an argument or build your case for your key point.

THE KEY POINT

- **Transition into the point**: A quick line to signal that you're broadening out to a more general point. For example, "And all this got me wondering…", or "So why am I telling you this?"

- **The wider point**: what's the lesson or key takeaway point you want to leave them with?

THE RELEVANCE

- **Relate it to them**: Tell them why this is important to them.

- **(Optional) Relate it to you personally**: How does the wider point affect you, on a personal level? This is a good chance to slip in one or two favourable facts about yourself, to help people get to know you better.

- **(Optional) Relate it to something you're selling**. This can be a product, a service, your category in general (e.g. "thank heavens she had insurance!"), or just an idea that forms a part of your key philosophy (e.g. "That's why it's vital that we all buy organic meat.")

- **(Optional) Relate it to a specific offer**: Perhaps you have a special offer or discount that you can somehow link back to this. Be careful here though: it's very easy to come across as too crass, too commercial, too self-serving, or to make it feel that the only point of the whole article was to lead in to a sales pitch. If in doubt, leave this part out.

- **Final line**: some kind of pithy, concise closing summary, leaving the reader with one final parting shot. It's important to include this, or the article will feel incomplete.

- **Cliff-hangers**: For bonus points, at some place where it naturally fits, add one or two cliff-hangers, to be resolved in a future issue of the newsletter.

When you're thinking of what to write, you can start with whichever part of the Situation—Key Point—Relevance formula you think of first, and then fill in the other parts. You could start with the event or story and then figure out the wider point, or you can start with the wider point and find a few stories or facts to back it up.

At first, writing this way might seem a bit self-indulgent or pompous. After all, who are *you* to preach? Well, it might feel strange to you at first, but it tends to feel quite natural to the reader, because they instinctively know that this is how people in authority communicate. And by publishing a newsletter, you *are* now an authority.

It will probably take you two or three attempts at writing the personal piece before you feel comfortable. That's fine, because it's not a natural type of writing that most of us do, so it takes time to find your feet.

Example Personal Piece

[THE SITUATION]

[Teaser opening] Have you ever had one of those days where you end up questioning the bigger things in life?

[Story] As you might know, I'm a private pilot, and I fly small aircraft out of Cambridge airport. Also based at the airport is the air ambulance helicopter, operated by a charity that I support. It's the same helicopter that Prince William, the Duke of Cambridge, used to fly until a few years ago.

So there I was, coming in to land, when air traffic control told me to circle around so that the air ambulance could take off. I heard the pilot of that yellow helicopter on the radio, announcing that he was taking off, and I saw him slowly rising up off the ground. He was using the callsign "HeliMed 88 Alpha", where the Alpha means that it's genuine emergency call, not a practice drill.

A minute later, I heard him on the radio again, this time saying he was landing because he'd been "stood down". Whenever I fly, I hear the air ambulance on the radio talking to the control tower a lot, but I've never heard him being stood down before.

The first thought that went through my head is that the patient might well have died at the scene of the accident, and so the air ambulance was no longer needed. What a sad thought. Somebody woke up this morning, perhaps planning an exciting day, maybe a meal tonight with their family, and yet they never made it.

[Related fact] Added to that, around five people a day get killed on our roads, often through no fault of their own.

[THE KEY POINT]

[Transition into the point] It just goes to show: you never know how long you've got left, so you've got to make the most of the time you've got.

Heavy stuff. Anyone who knows me will tell you that I'm a cheerful optimist by nature, and that was quite a sobering story. So let's turn this around and look at the positives.

[The wider point] What would you do if you knew you only had a year left to achieve everything you wanted to do? Would you waste time playing that silly game on your phone, or watching rubbish on the television just to "kill time"?

No. You wouldn't be trying to kill time, you'd be making the absolute most of it.

Happily, most of us will have much more than a year left to live, all being well, but if we can take that mindset—that time is precious and not to be wasted—and apply it to our own lives today, we could do so many more of the things that truly make us happy.

[THE RELEVANCE]

[Relate it to them] The truth is, we can all choose to be more intentional about how we fill our days.

So how would you choose to spend your time, if you knew your time was limited? (And unless you plan to live forever, in some sense, your time is always limited.)

[Relate it to me personally] For me, that would be reading books, flying the plane, playing the piano, and making sure I spend genuine quality time with Victoria. Now I think about it, perhaps we should book a week's holiday so we can get away and just relax together. I'll let you know where we decide to go: I've got something special that I'm cooking up for her birthday!

[Relate it to something I'm selling] One of the other things I love to do, of course, is to teach on the topics that I feel passionately about, and where I've spent a lot of time building up my knowledge and skills.

That's why, as I was musing on all this in the safety of the clubhouse at the aero club after I landed, I decided to dedicate next month to producing a brand new, hands-on, done-with-you course showing how you can launch a profitable newsletter in just 14 days.

I also think it will be fun to add in some daily coaching calls, to make sure that every single business owner who takes the course has their questions answered and ends up with a profitable newsletter.

[Relate it to a specific offer] Anyway, if this sounds like it might appeal to you, just hit "reply" to this newsletter, and I'll send you the details.

[Final line] Until next month, stay safe, and—please—use your time wisely.

Commentary on the example personal piece

This personal piece was about 700 words. It could be slimmed down, but I wanted to show you all the parts of the formula. It would make a good front page of a printed newsletter, and we'd replace the "hit reply" call-to-action at the end with a link to a website. In a slightly shortened form, it would work well as the personal piece at the start of an email newsletter.

Notice that I managed to get a lot of personal facts into this story. You now know that I fly planes, and that I also like to read books and play the piano. You know that I'm an optimist. You know that I'm a fan of using my time wisely. You know I value my relationship with my partner, and you know her name. You know that I support the air ambulance charity.

Not only are those things true, but they're also suggesting a bigger picture, namely the image of me that I'd like you to have: that I'm probably slightly more towards the cautious and responsible side of things than the crazy side of things! Since my business revolves around producing and sending marketing materials for companies, I need clients to feel that they can trust me. If this story revolved around getting involved in a bar-room brawl, where the bar stools are flying and the beer bottles are smashing, it wouldn't quite create the same impression.

I could have chosen to end this personal piece before the [Relate it to something I'm selling] section, and jumped straight to the final line. However, I chose to do a soft sell, introducing a new product by simply explaining what I'm planning.

I gave a couple of features: it's a course with daily coaching calls. I gave a specific benefit: get your questions answered. I gave a specific outcome: launch a profitable newsletter in 14 days. I also related it to a specific offer, but in a very low-key way ("just hit reply"). Nothing too pushy, but to somebody who might be interested, there's enough meat to at least pique their interest and perhaps ask in advance for details. It's really like a "coming soon" movie trailer.

I managed to throw in a soap opera cliffhanger too, regarding the holiday, when I wrote, "I'll let you know where we decide to go: I've got something special that I'm cooking up for her birthday!" Admittedly, it's not quite up there with "Who Shot J.R.?", but it's at least creating some sort of anticipation by putting a thought in that person's mind that I might choose to go back to in the next issue. (They call these half-stories "open loops" in NLP, if you're familiar with that.)

Incidentally, I went back and added that cliffhanger right after I'd finished the first draft, I didn't put it in from the start.

The key point I want you to notice from this example is that it's not perfect. It could be better. I deliberately left it as a first draft, to show you how these personal pieces get built.

In the second draft, I'd polish it further. It could be shorter, more punchy, more powerful. The sentences themselves could be a bit shorter. The main point feels a little clichéd and might need a bit more of a unique spin. I could hook the wider point more directly to the specific things that my audience is seeking to achieve (making sales: building their business and growing their wealth by serving more people).

The cliff-hanger could be more intriguing or more directly related to something the reader is desperate to know (although at the bottom of the newsletter we can achieve some of those aims with a teaser for what's "Coming up next month…").

So it's not perfect, but it's good enough. "Done beats perfect", as they say. You could send this out and get results. It certainly beats sending a blank page! It touches on a lot of the things it needs to touch on. It probably strikes roughly the right balance between blowing my own trumpet without being too self-indulgent or arrogant. If it's going to the right people, it will stimulate some sales interest too.

Ideas for Relationship content and the personal piece

1. *Vital*: the personal piece itself: a personal introduction or letter from the boss (you!).

2. Credentials of your team, e.g. qualifications awarded to your team, society memberships.

3. Meet our customer-support team: here are the people who will take good care of you.

4. Photos of you or your people getting up to something fun.

5. New employees joining your company.

6. Personal messages wishing readers well, at Christmas, New Year, Easter, etc.

7. Recruitment: if you're looking for new people, an existing customer or prospect might be ideal.

8. Profiles of your suppliers. This can be a proper snooze-fest if you don't do it right, so you want to turn it into a behind-the-scenes look at how they work their magic.

9. Topical comments on current affairs or cultural happenings (hopefully not contentious or controversial—steer clear of religion and politics if at all possible).

10. Staff picks of products or services that they like.

11. Your family.

12. Things that you love.

13. Things that you dislike, or pet peeves.

14. Your hobbies.

15. Things you find inspiring or interesting.

16. Human interest stories.

17. Photos of pets, belonging to you or your team.

18. Spotlight on an employee, with an interview, perhaps with a photograph (personally I don't like calling this "Employee of the Month", because it implies all the other employees are in some way inferior).

19. Your holidays.

20. Your friends.

21. Profiles of your employees.

22. A thank-you to your customers, patients, donors, staff, etc.

23. Wedding, birth, death, retirement of people you know, or customers (with their permission).

24. A day/week in the life of a certain team member. This can focus more on facts and become What-you-do content, or it can focus more on the human and emotional side and become Relationship content to bond the reader with the people in your organisation.

CHAPTER 17

Community-building content

You want people to feel that they are included, and that they are part of a successful tribe that revolves around you. This bonds them to you, and helps you keep those customers for far longer than you otherwise would, while also helping to keep competitors from luring them away. That's what Community-building content does.

Ideas for Community-building content

1. Question of the month: ask a question to get replies and feedback from your readers. You can then hopefully incorporate this into the next issue, talking about what you learned.

2. Stories of how people first came to do business with you (the aim is to push prospects off the fence, to get them to take the plunge and become customers for the first time).

3. Customer case study showing a success—see if you can find something interesting or unusual that is in some way remarkable.

4. Customer testimonial for how you have helped them.

5. Crowd-funded campaigns that you are running or supporting.

6. Asking your customers to review you on various online sites such as TripAdvisor or Amazon.

7. Letters from readers (including emails, tweets, and Facebook messages), sometimes with further comments from you. Readers often like to see their name in print, but get their permission first or use something vague like "Mr J Smith from London".

8. Reviews of your products, written by customers. You can get these from Amazon (or other sites), but remember that Amazon holds the copyright on reviews, so you can only use small snippets of them.

9. Mentioning a customer in passing. The aim here is to build a cast of minor characters around you, like a soap opera, and show that you are influential in your community. It's really just name-dropping!

10. Charity or non-profit contributions or activities that you or your team are involved in, either personally or on behalf of the company.

11. Local initiatives, such as a "Save our high street" campaign. Even if you're not actually on the high street it can still be good to get involved with this sort of thing, as long as you don't come across as a glory-hunter, because it positions you as a company that cares about your community.

12. Local news that affects your area, your readers' area, or your business.

13. Photos of customers.

14. Welcoming new customers.

15. Reviews of your company from sites such as Google, Feefo, Trustpilot, or TripAdvisor.

16. Local community events that you will be taking part in, or have already taken part in, sponsored, etc.

17. Before-and-after stories of how you have helped people.

18. Announce the winners of your competitions. Check you have their permission to use their names, otherwise do this in an abbreviated form that doesn't directly identify any individuals.

19. Profiles of your customers and their businesses.

CHAPTER 18

Sales content

In a newsletter, Sales content is the art of selling without selling! Or rather, without being seen to be selling. If you come across as pushy or like a salesperson, you lose the aura that your newsletter is a publication and not a marketing piece. That said, there is plenty that you can mention.

Ideas for Sales content

1. A free course or seminar that you're offering (online or in person) as a way to bring new people into the business, or to sell them a product or service.

2. Giveaways of merchandise, e.g. a free hat or umbrella with your logo on it.

3. Announcing a new publication: a book, special report, audio recording, video, webinar, or something else you are providing as part of a marketing effort.

4. "Free gift with purchase" offer.

5. Free resources and information that you are offering, such as a book.

6. Promotional giveaways.

7. A non-salesy spotlight on a non-competing nearby business, especially if they can return the favour somehow, perhaps distributing your newsletter in their place of business (because they're featured in the issue).

8. Announcing a new product.

9. Coupons for discounts—coupons are more effective if they have a deadline and expire soon, to stimulate urgency.

10. Announcing a new service you are offering.

11. A competition tied to enquiries or sales—be aware of the legal aspects of running a competition.

12. A promotional discount.

13. A special offer or coupon exclusively for readers of the newsletter.

14. Invitation for someone to consider becoming a distributor, franchisee, or otherwise involved in your business.

15. Mentioning another company to promote their product or service, with some kind of reciprocal deal where they will at some point promote you to their audience.

16. Information on your customer loyalty scheme, and an invitation to join it.

17. Announcement of a new or updated piece of marketing that you're doing, such as a newly designed website, launching a new blog or a new podcast.

18. Customer appreciation events you are holding.

19. A new distributor that people can now buy through.

20. Early-bird offers that make people feel special, like they're part of the in-crowd.

21. Invitations to events you are running.

22. "Free gift just for turning up" offer (such as a gift voucher for taking a test drive of a car, or for coming into your office).

23. Invitations to special behind-the-scenes access.

24. How to find recordings of past events or webinars that you have been involved with, which contain some kind of sales message.

Through-the-door offers: a magic technique

Try running what I call a "through-the-door" offer. It's an offer deliberately designed with the sole intention of getting customers through the door, so that you can then sell them something else.

A great example is a garden centre cafe near me, which includes plenty of coupons in its newsletter for a free hot drink, which includes the fancy coffees. This has got my partner Victoria and me through the door and into that garden centre dozens of times!

While we're there getting our drink, we're also buying food in the cafe, then buying other products in the garden centre too. Over the years, we must have spent hundreds of pounds in there as a result—maybe even thousands!

There's another nice garden centre cafe about a minute down the road, but because of this great through-the-door offer from the first place, we're magnetically attracted there! This is an amazing technique, and you should really think hard about how you can incorporate it into your business.

The drink costs them a few pennies, yet has led to their cafe being constantly packed with people, and it all starts with a great through-the-door offer in their newsletter.

CHAPTER 19

What-they-like content

You should include some information that is not directly related to what you do, or the industry you're in, but is more about what your customers will like, based on their demographics (who they are) and psychographics (what they're interested in). For example, if you're in B2B (selling to businesses), a lot of your readers are likely to be into personal development, motivation, and self-improvement.

You've really got to know your audience here. What some groups would enjoy, others would consider irrelevant.

Ideas for What-they-like content

1. "Pick of the month" in some interesting category.
2. Links to interesting books and articles, in a "What we're reading" section.
3. Editorial: what do you think about a certain topic, news article, or issue outside your industry?
4. A round-up of useful or interesting pictures and photos from the web.

5. Gift guides for products outside of your industry, that you don't personally sell. For example, if your readers are mostly professional men in their fifties, there's a chance a fair few of them will like golf.

6. Fascinating facts about topics that will be of interest to your readers.

7. Health topics, particularly if there is some kind of tie-in either to you personally or to your industry, for example "I suffered from this condition and here's what I found", or "10 ways office workers can beat stress". Make sure it's clear you're not a doctor (unless you actually are one!).

8. Apps, software, websites, or tools that you enjoy using.

9. Tips on aspects of life outside of work.

10. Reviews of products, books, films, etc. that your customers are likely to be interested in.

11. General consumer news that will be of interest to lots of people.

12. Predictions for the year ahead, outside of your industry— either serious or deliberately light-hearted.

CHAPTER 20

Referral content

The three core benefits of a newsletter are sales, retention, and referrals. Therefore, it should come as no surprise that Referral content should be included in your newsletter.

A referral is simply word-of-mouth marketing: getting your existing customers and readers to recommend you, your products and services, to other people.

The people most likely to refer others to you are your biggest fans. They're your most loyal customers, the customers who buy the most often, and the customers who are best-suited to your business. That's great, because people tend to know other people who are similar to themselves, so effectively **you're cloning your best customers!**

For referrals in newsletters, there are two people involved: the person doing the referring, and the person being referred. This means you have two goals:

1. **Pass it on**: get your original reader to recommend you.

2. **Join my list**: Bring this new person into your fold.

Bringing someone new into your fold could include them joining your list (with their permission to market to them), making an enquiry with you, or making a purchase.

Referral marketing is a much wider topic than I've got space to cover in this book. Indeed, it would be at least a book all by itself. However, in this chapter I can give you a few recommendations.

Make sure you're good enough to be recommended

It should go without saying that in order for somebody to recommend you, they have to at least be satisfied (preferably happy or jumping for joy) with your products and services, your customer service, your price, and the overall experience of doing business with you. As marketer Seth Godin might say, to be remarked upon, you've got to be remarkable. For me, the key point is that they can't be embarrassed to recommend you, or they won't!

I'm going to assume that you have enough readers and customers that would fall into this category of being willing to recommend you. If you don't, fix it fast!

As a side point: if you're not sure how many people would recommend you, or you want to track and improve the number of people who would recommend you, look at the Net Promoter methodology. You can get the basics on Net Promoter (also known as Net Promoter Score) from Wikipedia, or see the Net Promoter website at www.netpromotersystem.com.

(Net Promoter and NPS are registered trademarks of Bain & Company, Inc., Satmetrix Systems, Inc., and Fred Reichheld.)

Essentially it involves asking the question "How likely is it that you would recommend our company/product/service to a friend or colleague?". You've probably seen that question in quite a few customer surveys, and the NPS methodology is the reason.

Reasons why people will recommend you

One of the secrets of success of businesses that have lots of referrals is simply that they keep reminding their customers to refer others. People are often happy to refer you to others, they just forget.

At the heart of any kind of recommendation is some sort of "reason why" that person would recommend you *right now*.

We can consider the urgent referral and the non-urgent referral:

Urgent referral: "My kitchen is flooded, can you recommend me a plumber who can get here in the next ten minutes?"

Non-urgent referral: "Can you recommend a plumber who might be able to work on my new kitchen next year?"

In the case of the flooded kitchen—the urgent referral—your best bet is to be top-of-mind of the person being asked, and keeping yourself top-of-mind is something a regular newsletter can help with.

In the case of the non-urgent referral, there needs to be a "reason why" to make the referral happen. Why should your reader refer you to someone else *today*?

Referral offers and rewarded referrals

The "reason why" usually comes down to some kind of offer that you make, so let's look at a few types of offer.

The most basic kind of referral offer is the offer of the newsletter itself. If you can get your reader to find your newsletter valuable, they might know other people who will value the information and who would like to subscribe.

Another kind of referral offer is "bring a friend". This can work well for local businesses who host customer appreciation events. For example, you might host a summer fête to thank your customers, and ask your customers to bring a friend, whose details you can then capture (making sure you get their permission to market to them).

A good solid way to get referrals quickly is to use a "member get member" offer. This is a promotion where we give an existing reader or customer a special offer that they can use for their friend. The offer is usually some kind of exclusive discount, exclusive product, exclusive service, or exclusive bundle that's offered only as part of a referral promotion.

The benefits of the offer can be one-sided, so only the friend gets a benefit, or it can be two-sided, where both the referrer (your original customer) and their friend both get a benefit.

An example of a **one-sided referral offer** that got quick results is a pet food company that ran an advertisement offering a free trial of their customised food, when you just pay £2 for delivery. We took them up on the offer, and the food arrived along with some coupons to give to a friend. The coupon gave the same offer of the free food, but this time paying just £1 delivery charge. We have friends with pets, because as I said earlier, people tend to know people who are like them. We gave the coupon to a friend, who then tried the food on their dog. Within less than a week, we'd gone from never having heard of the company to being a customer and referring another customer. That's the power of a referral offer.

Note that this was a one-sided offer: the benefit was solely to our friend, and all we got as the people doing the referring was the warm glow and the coolness factor of being the person doing the recommending (which shouldn't be underestimated).

An example of a **two-sided referral offer** is a television company telling their customers: "Recommend us to a friend, and if they sign up and stay with us for a month you'll each get £30 off your next bill". Another example is the Dropbox online computer file storage system, which runs an offer "Invite friends to Dropbox and you'll both earn extra storage space".

The incentive can be cash, discounts, extra services like Dropbox is offering, or it can be a product or a gift voucher of some kind. If you're selling to businesses, where it's not the prospect's own money they're spending, a special product, gift, or Amazon gift voucher can work better than a discount.

Rewards to your existing customer, the person doing the referring, don't have to be based on money. You can also offer something that doesn't cost you anything (e.g. a free PDF or video), a free call with you, promotional gear, or mentions in your newsletter. The key is knowing your reader so that you can offer them something they will value.

Things to include in your newsletter to stimulate referrals

Earlier in this chapter, I said there are two goals your newsletter needs to achieve with referrals: get somebody to pass on your newsletter, and then capture the new person onto your list with permission to market to them.

Let's look first at what to say to your existing reader. You can include a section in your email newsletter that says something like:

- "Do you know someone who should be getting this newsletter? Forward it on to them, so they don't miss out."
- "Finding this newsletter valuable? Pass it on to a friend."
- "We grow our business by referrals. Feel free to forward this email to anyone who you think would find it useful."

You can include gentle reminders in your newsletter, for example at some point in an article you can say:

- "If you know anyone who's had a problem like this, feel free to pass on this newsletter to them, so that this article can help them"

- ■ "If you know someone who's facing a similar issue, ask them to give me a call, because I can probably help them."
- ■ "If you've got a friend that also needs (something), please tell them about me, so I can give them the same fantastic (something) at an affordable price."

This last example is a bit more salesy. Don't sell too hard though, or you'll lose your status as a trusted publisher.

You can also include social media buttons in an email newsletter, for Facebook, Twitter, email forwarding, etc. I recommend trying these buttons, tracking the results, and if they don't work particularly well for you then stop including them and use the space for something else.

Things to include in your newsletter to capture the person being referred

Once you've got somebody to forward your newsletter to a friend, or to give a printed copy of your newsletter to a friend, the next vital step is to make sure that new person takes action. Assuming that person is in some way qualified to be a customer of yours, we want that person to join your list.

If they make a purchase or an enquiry immediately then you probably have systems in place for capturing their details and making sure you have permission to market to them. (If you don't, you need to sort it out!)

But if the new person doesn't immediately enquire—and most people won't—then we need your newsletter itself to tell them how they can join your list. We can optionally give an incentive for them to do so.

The most basic kind of text we can include in an email newsletter to do this job is along the lines of:

- "If you were forwarded this newsletter, click here for a free subscription." (in an email newsletter)
- "For your free subscription to this newsletter, go to www. NewsletterExpert.com today." (in a printed newsletter).

You can sweeten the deal a bit by giving a reason to subscribe. This could be promoting the contents of the newsletter, promoting discounts contained within the newsletter, or promoting something free that comes when someone signs up, such as a free report or free video. (These free pieces are often called lead magnets.)

For example:

- "Sign up to our newsletter to receive exclusive weekly offers only available to our subscribers."
- "Get 20% off your first order, and free shipping, when you sign up to our newsletter."
- "Subscribe to our newsletter and get your free guide to (something exciting and intriguing)."

CHAPTER 21

Fun content

The idea of including fun content might seem frivolous, or a waste of space, but it most definitely is not. It is put there very deliberately. Why? To encourage people to open up the newsletter and read it.

After all, if the newsletter doesn't get read, it can't achieve many of its major strategic objectives. (It's still not a complete dead duck though—even the act of a customer seeing the newsletter will remind them of you, and give you a little more brand recognition and top-of-mind awareness.)

So don't ignore fun content, but figure out how to do something that your customers will enjoy.

What sorts of fun content can you include?

1. Cartoons that specifically accompany your article, to help make a point. (Be sure to get copyright clearance, don't just paste them off the internet or you'll be in trouble!).

2. Cartoons that stand alone, either to make a point or just to be funny in a way that's completely unrelated to what you do.

3. Quizzes. These are often seen in magazines. They can be a test of general knowledge, or a test of subject-specific knowledge (such as the impossibly hard Formula 1 quiz in *Autosport* magazine!). Alternatively, they can be a personality-assessment sort of quiz, where there are no real right or wrong answers. These can be serious, or funny things like "What kind of dog are you?"

4. Inspirational quotes. I like to include "Words of Wisdom" at the top of an email newsletter. Be careful with quoting song lyrics, because the copyright enforcers can be pretty hot on those!

5. Fascinating facts. This is weird stuff that people might think "Well I never knew that!" Sometimes you can spin these out into "Weird World" articles.

6. Humorous short articles that claim to be written by your dog, cat, or some kind of inanimate object. They can often carry a message that is helpful to you (such as a sales message), but very much look like they are *not* about sales!

7. Jokes. Keep them clean!

8. Funny pictures, images, and memes—remember copyright again!

Puzzles should probably stay in print only

Some types of fun content, such as puzzles, are much easier to do in print. You can include all sorts of puzzles, such as a crossword, word search, maze, sudoku, or any of the newer puzzle formats that come out of Japan with alarming regularity. It's not really worth putting these in an email, because they are too hard to complete on a screen.

CHAPTER 22

Mistakes to avoid

While it's possible to do a newsletter very well, it's also possible to fall into a few bear traps.

When I analyse newsletters that are sent to me, here are the most common problems I find:

- Being boring—usually caused by focusing too much on What-you-do content and not enough on the remainder of the Captivating Categories of Content™ and building a relationship with the reader. Note that an interesting topic doesn't always equal interesting writing.

- Not including the personal piece. Even if it's short, it *must* be there. Many of the major strategic objectives of a newsletter are achieved using the personal piece.

- Not sending the newsletter to as many people as you can afford to reach (you can be selective in who you send it to).

- Not actively promoting your newsletter to keep it positioned as a must-read piece of communication with an ever-growing audience.

- Not giving enough time and attention to create a high-quality product.

- Unsuitable graphic design—it doesn't have to be fancy, but it does have to match your other marketing and your overall image.

- Sloppy production values: low-quality images, lots of typos, grammatical mistakes.

- Content that doesn't suit your audience.

- Turning the newsletter into a promotional pitch-fest full of hardcore selling and not enough information.

- Having adverts from other companies in your newsletter.

- Giving up too soon—one edition of a newsletter is a great place to start, but it's the long-term publishing that will really make sure you achieve all the strategic objectives of your newsletter.

- Irregular timing. Your newsletter needs to go out on a regular schedule, so that people come to expect it.

- Inconsistent design or layout. Use the same basic template and structure every time, so that your newsletter is instantly recognisable to regular readers.

How to get started

Congratulations, you've made it to the end of the book! That shows that you're serious about creating a high-quality newsletter that will help you to grow your business and keep your customers for longer.

You're now left with one key question to answer:

When are you going to get started?

They say that the best time to plant a tree was 100 years ago; the second-best time is now!

The longer you have your newsletter, the more benefits it can give you.

What would it feel like if you could get your first issue in front of customers in just a couple of weeks from now? What would having a great newsletter mean to your business? What would it mean for you personally?

If a newsletter could transform your business, and perhaps even transform your life, would you take that first step?

Make a decision to go full speed ahead and put this amazing marketing method to work for you, starting *today*.

Here are the first few actions you can take:

1. Set a date for when you want your first issue to be finished and sent to customers.

2. Decide who will write the newsletter and put it all together. Will you write it yourself? Can you delegate it?

3. Write down the first few steps you will take. This is the start of your plan.

4. Put the plan into action!

"I just want to get it done!"

Need to get your newsletter done the fast and easy way? I work with selected clients to write and distribute their monthly newsletter, in email or in print. To apply for a Strategy Session to see if we could work together, visit:

www.NewsletterExpert.com/call

APPENDIX 1

Why work with me, rather than writing your newsletter yourself?

By now, you might be wondering whether you should write your newsletter yourself, or hire me to write it and send it out for you (with you checking and approving it, of course, and having as much or as little input as your wish).

Let me ask you something: do you really think that if you decide to do it yourself, it will actually get done? Starting soon? And done every single month without fail? Or will it be one of those things that gets pushed down the list, left until the last minute, and then rushed, and eventually abandoned despite the sales it's making?

It takes a long time to produce a great newsletter, and I'm not going to lie, it's hard work, even if you're coordinating various freelancers.

If you work with me, I guarantee that it will actually get done! And it will be done to a proper professional standard. I could get your first issue out there and making sales for you in just a couple of weeks from now.

So maybe you think you can get it done every month, but you're not sure what to write about. They say that you can't see the picture if you're in the frame, and sometimes it can take an outside eye to find what's interesting to your readers. I can find plenty of interesting things to put into your newsletter, based on my experience and my proven formulas and techniques, like the ones I've shown you in this book.

Or maybe you don't think of yourself as a great writer, and your talents lie elsewhere. Why sweat blood over something you'll struggle with, when you could delegate it to me and free up your own time to use your own super-powers? You could use this time to work directly with your clients where you can personally add the most value—or you can use the extra time to relax!

I can see evolving best practice and "what's working now" across different companies, so I can get you better results than you'd get on your own. I continue to carefully study how newsletters and similar marketing communications are evolving, to make sure that my clients remain able to profitably use newsletters in their business.

And finally, since I literally wrote the book on the 32 major strategic objectives of a newsletter, I can help you to determine your own key objectives, then keep a balanced eye on what's going into your newsletter to make sure that you achieve your goals.

So if you want all the great benefits of a newsletter, without having to write it yourself, in less than 30 minutes a month, arrange a call with me and let's see if we can work together.

Visit www.NewsletterExpert.com/call to get started, and I'll talk to you soon.

PLEASE REVIEW THIS BOOK

If you have enjoyed this book...

If you have enjoyed this book, I would be very grateful if you would please leave a review for me on Amazon or wherever you purchased it.

This will help other business owners just like you to find this book and benefit from the amazing power of a newsletter.

And remember: if you spot any "typos", they're just British English! ☺

Thank you very much.

Download your FREE quick-start video and time-saving tools

Quick-start video
A summary of this entire book in just 30 minutes.

"The Perfect Newsletter" Checklist
Tick these boxes to make sure your newsletter gets you more sales, retention, and referrals.

"Article Idea Finder" Cheat Sheet
How to get your first 10 article ideas in 10 minutes.

Pre-Flight "Fingers-Crossed" Checklist
The essential final review before sending your newsletter to avoid embarrassing mistakes.

Your questions answered—20 page bonus chapter
FAQ information that changes regularly, included as a free download so it's always up to date. Includes:

- How often should I send my newsletter?
- How can I sell directly from my newsletter?
- Which email software should I use?
- What's a good open rate for an email newsletter?
- How do I keep my newsletter out of the spam folder and the Gmail promotions tab?

Get your FREE video and bonuses now, at
www.NewsletterExpert.com/bonus

INDEX

Made in the USA
Middletown, DE
02 August 2023

36100344R00106